C. RUTH TAYLOR

FOREWORD BY
DR. DONOVAN THOMAS

KEYS TO WIN AT LIFE

100 PROVEN WAYS
TO HANDLE LIFE'S CHALLENGES

Extra MILE Innovators

A GIFT FOR:

_____

FROM:

_____

To equip you to win at life

ON

_____

.   .   .   .   .

Published by
Extra MILE Innovators
21 Phoenix Avenue,
Kingston 10, Jamaica W.I.
www.extramileja.com
administrator@extramileja.com
Tele: (1876) 782-9893

.   .   .   .   .

Illustrations by
Lika Kvirikashvili

Cover Design, Print Layout & eBook by
N.D. Author Services [NDAS]
www.NDAuthorServices.com

To a great friend, Tedecia Powell-Coley,
On whom and through whom
I have been able to test the veracity,
effectiveness
And power of many of these keys

. . . . .

To all who will use these keys to win at life

ENDORSEMENTS

Keys to Win at Life is a must read, a very useful resource for every library and every person who values discipline, character formation and self-management. This well-written resource provides exposure of common issues and meaningful techniques not commonly treated in this unique way—incorporating well known proverbs to highlight the cultural fusion. This book is a "road map" for life. It is authentic, coming from the heart of the writer—"If fish com from riba bottom an tell yu sey shark dung deh believe im" [If fish comes from river bottom and tells you shark is down there, believe him].

Its breath and scope employ keys of attitude and actions, decision and design, identity and investments, relationships and resources to ensure the usefulness of the book.

All readers, whatever their world-view, will find in this book much to stimulate, enhance, and restructure their thinking at self-management and acceptance of life inevitables with confidence for solution.

Any parent who is concerned about the all-round development of the child will treasure this book and will do well to place a copy in the hand of the child on the 13th birthday.

Keys to Win at Life is no ordinary book and demands your careful attention; a must-have —a must win.

Dr. Hyacinth Peart
Family Counsellor

.   .   .   .   .

Drawing from her own life and noteworthy advice from others, Cameka "Ruth" Taylor provides highly readable, concise, accessible and practical statements about being successful at life. Ruth provides these superb keys in written form, and her productive life is a testament to following these keys. Read the book, implement the keys and see positive changes in your life.

Jeremy Griffin, Ph.D.
Global Outreach Coordinator at Covenant Church

.   .   .   .   .

Anyone involved with life's challenges, who desires to effectively absorb their lessons and/or resolve them, will treasure this book. The writer's innovative approach in utilizing the wisdom of a harvest of proverbs is invaluable and appropriate for readers of all ages. The passion behind this book emanates from one who is committed to helping others face difficulties through practical and novel means. She desires that those who benefit from it will give all the glory to God.

Joan Pinkney
Counselling Psychologist and Lecturer

FOREWORD

I do consider it a privilege and an honour to be invited to write the Foreword for this the third publication by Cameka (Ruth) Taylor, **KEYS TO WIN AT LIFE: 100 Proven Ways to Handle Life's Challenges**.

My association with Ruth spans almost two (2) decades. It has been a joy to watch her grow from strength to strength over these years. I am very delighted to express my congratulations to Ruth for joining the distinguished group of authors who have written not just one or two books, but a third! Ruth's life story is a series of challenges and even despair that have caused her to dig deep, to think wide, and to find creative strategies to overcome the obstacles that life throws at her. Her ability to press through misfortunes is a testimony to her determination, resilience, and passion to succeed, even under unfavourable conditions.

This book captures 100 strategies, many of which the author has practised herself, in order to develop a winning approach to life. In addition, other strategies have been gleaned from examining the lives of successful people and by reviewing the literary work of experts. The keys presented in this book have relevance and application for people of all ages, nationalities, social and educational standing. I encourage you to delve in; read in any order you desire, and be enriched, inspired and empowered to live a more meaningful and fulfilled life.

As you read this book, I challenge you not to keep these keys of success to yourself but to think about five persons you know who would benefit from the wisdom, principles, guidelines and recommendations contained in this book. Be sure to recommend this book to them, so that they can find greater empowerment for greater success in life!

Again, congratulations to Cameka (Ruth) Taylor for demonstrating and documenting keys to success. Your commitment to excellence and hard work, accompanied by your constant smiles, continues to be an inspiration. I wish you every success.

Dr. Donovan Thomas
President and Founder,
Choose Life International

TABLE OF CONTENTS

INTRODUCTION

"Life is a daring adventure or nothing at all."
—Helen Keller

Dare to Win

The newborn cried as the doctor spanked his bottom to stimulate him to take his first breath. What a way to be introduced to the world! After surviving the race of 350 million sperms to be conceived, and nine months nestled inside his mother's womb, pain was his introduction to the world. The baby's mother struggled and pushed; she pushed past the pain to give birth. She was guided expertly by those trained and skilled in the art of delivery, and after a safe delivery, she was mesmerized at the sight of her beautiful baby boy. He was worth all the pain, after all. He was a desire fulfilled and for this, her heart was very glad, because she was well aware that sometimes, some mothers and some babies don't make it.

The baby's entrance into the world is noteworthy and is indicative of life on planet Earth. His welcome spanking is indicative of what life will and can do to you. The mother's experience reminds us that in life there will be moments of pain but also moments of joy, and we will need the help and guidance of others to overcome the pain and manoeuvre life safely. In Jamaica we say: "If you want good, your nose afi run," which means any worthwhile pursuit or goal will involve hard work, discipline and some pain, so aptly portrayed by the birthing process.

When the baby arrived, he did not receive a life map to guide him on his earthly journey. He had no instructions on how to live successfully, and if his parents fail to teach him, he will be off to a bad start. If his schools fail to teach him or he fails to follow proper instructions and guidance, the journey will be even more challenging. If he follows the wrong company and bad advice, he may end up an early fatality or live an unfruitful life. Proper guidance at an early age will help him to travel well on this journey called "life". He will need key life strategies and skills, through direct and indirect training, to overcome the pain and challenges that life will bring. Beating the odds will be difficult but not impossible.

Our life-winning keys book will certainly help this baby and many others to beat the odds and weather the storms of life. It is geared towards equipping you with key life skills and strategies, success principles and resources to boldly face life and win. The many keys that are included here remind me of the large bunch of keys often seen in the caretaker's possession. Sometimes these keys are not labelled, but he knows which key opens each door of the facility. In this book, we have labelled the keys to assist you in finding the right one to unlock the solution to your problem. Beware that a key which resembles another may not be the right one for your challenge. However, over time, you too, like the caretaker, will learn to differentiate between them. These keys will give you insights and reasons to keep breathing and winning when times get hard.

Now, are you ready to *live to win?* Are you ready to succeed despite the odds? Are you ready to push past hurt and pain to give birth to your dreams? It is my wish that you will not abort your journey because of the pain and the obstacles. I believe you can win at life! In fact, I double dare you to win at life! I double dare you to live a purposeful, productive and profitable life despite the odds!

SECTION I: UNDERSTANDING THE KEYS

A nuh ebreeting soak up waata a sponge
[It is not everything that soaks up water is a sponge]
—Jamaican Proverb

THE STORY BEHIND THE KEYS

If you falter in a time of trouble,
how small is your strength!
—Bible Proverb

In May 2016, my mother and I were interviewed on Television Jamaica's popular morning show, "Smile Jamaica," and the interviewer, Neville Bell, commented that "I seem to be a very confident individual." His unforgettable statement is evidence of my dramatic transformation, because I have not always been a confident or strong person. In fact, I was once a very weak, timid, purposeless, suicidal and defeated being, who hated problems and wanted to escape them every chance I got. The change to which Neville referred is the result of a serious life quest, which started at the age of seventeen (17) to find a reason to live.

At that time, I was experiencing a deep vacousness and disillusionment with life that propelled me on a quest to find a purpose for living. Later on in my quest, I was spurred by the need to find ways and means of living effectively and to help others to do the same. My quest yielded answers via a combination of the Christian Faith, psychology, personal development, my own failures and successes, as well as the stories of the failures and successes of others. It is these answers that infused me with the confidence, strength and hope that Neville evidently saw that morning.

Furthermore, in recent years, quite a number of persons have been coming to me with their life challenges or seeking my counsel regarding how to be more effective in their personal and professional lives. At times, I felt I was not equipped to help these persons; in order to assist them, I often evaluated my own life experiences for solutions and looked for the patterns and principles employed by other successful persons to treat-address such issues. I read extensively and listened repeatedly to the presentations of those who were helping others to solve similar life issues. In my research, I stumbled upon the teachings of author and business philosopher Jim Rohn, and his advice on treating problems has greatly influenced the compilation of these keys.

Rohn wisely said, "Don't wish it was easier; wish you were better. Don't wish for less problems; wish for more skills. Don't wish for less challenge; wish for more wisdom." These life life-winning keys and proverbs reflect the wisdom and skills needed to treat with problems.

The keys to win at life are problem-solving and success strategies to help you live an effective life and to get the most out of life—personally, relationally, professionally, intellectually, financially, emotionally and spiritually.

These 100 life-winning keys represent the most helpful answers from my personal odyssey and research on how to handle life's challenges. I have proven their effectiveness in my own life and with my clients. These keys are essential tools in my success kit as I seek to equip others to achieve their life goals. Furthermore, since I have personally experienced a great degree of transformation from using many of these keys, it is only fitting to pass them on to others. It is my hope that by sharing them, many lives locally (in Jamaica) and globally will be similarly transformed.

Note well that I have not yet mastered all 100 keys. However, I do intend to use them all throughout my life, because these are all proven keys, which I or others have used to win at life. Now with so many keys, I think you will want to know which key is the master key. Well, I believe the master problem-solving key is really a blended key of **studying and following models of success and winning with Faith.** Do further note that, although these life-winning keys are simple, they are not all easy to employ, but they are all necessary to win at life. Therefore, go right ahead and use these keys to win at life!

AIM AND BENEFITS

The aim of this book is to arm you for the day of adversity, to increase your strength and to equip you with strategies to succeed at life. These life-winning keys will enable you to W.I.N., that is, to do the following:

- ✔ **W**eather the storms of life
- ✔ **I**ntentionally plan for your success
- ✔ **Never** give up hope and **never** give up on life

WHO CAN USE THIS BOOK?

Fortune favours the prepared mind.
—Louis Pasteur

This book is a tool to be used by *all* who are looking for principles and strategies to live an effective life. The keys are not speculative theories but common sense principles and time tested success strategies. They are presented in a way to benefit children, youths and adults. This book is a tool to fuel your success at home, work, school and elsewhere. You can gift this book to others and recommend it especially to the following:

1. Family, friends, classmates and colleagues
2. Businesses and their affiliates
3. Educational institutions and non-profit organizations
4. Hospitals, churches, community groups and clubs
5. Guidance Counsellors and Career Development Officers

6. Persons in the helping professions
7. Personal development coaches, life skills specialists and mentors

HOW TO USE THIS BOOK

This book is a companion to the textbook, *Design to Win: A Road Map to Discover Your Purpose and the Keys to Win at Life*, which is used in my life skills coaching and personal development course known as "Design to Win." Three words should be borne in mind whenever you think of using this problem-solving and success tool: prevention, preparation and prescription. These are explained as follows:

Prevention: Familiarize yourself with the keys to avoid certain problems and pitfalls in life. Familiarize yourself with the keys and bear them in mind before you engage in any planning exercise, so that you can plan wisely and effectively.

Preparation: Don't wait until you have a problem before you refer to the keys. Study them and hide them in your heart to arm yourself with the knowledge to create a successful life and deal effectively with your own life challenges. Arm yourself beforehand with the knowledge to help others plan for their success and help them deal with their life challenges.

Prescription: Each time you or someone else faces a challenge, use the keys to unlock the solution to that problem. When you feel lost and in need of direction for your life, draw from the keys to help you find direction and purpose. Use them as a road map to get to your destination. Whenever you need principles to be more efficient or to develop yourself, your career, business or organization, use the appropriate life-winning keys. They are medicine for your soul and, like a doctor, you can prescribe the life-winning keys to your family, friends, co-workers and all those who desire to win at life.

KEY COMPOSITION AND ORGANIZATION

As mentioned previously, these life-winning keys have been gained from personal experience, careful study and observation drawn from the Bible; stories of highly successful people, and the literature and teachings of success experts like John Maxwell and Brian Tracy. The keys are organized around my D.A.I.R to Win problem-solving and strategic planning recipe, which has eight core ingredients for success. These ingredients are paired using each letter in the recipe. The D.A.I.R to Win recipe employs the journey metaphor in its application as follows:

Decision and Design: Before you take a journey or travel, decide where you want to go and why. Describe the destination as clearly as possible and design a strategic plan or route to get there.

Attitudes and Actions: Learn and adopt the right attitudes and actions along the journey. Try to follow the habits and practices of people who've taken the journey before you successfully.

Identity and Investment: Keep in mind your identity as you travel on your life journey and invest in yourself and others along the journey.

Relationships and Resources: Establish the right relationships; gather and manage the resources needed to make the journey a success.

The life-winning keys are described in two ways:

1. using the phrase "win with..." (*Win with Clarity)* and
2. using an action verb or phrase to describe the strategy, concept or technique required to win (*Beat Fear to Win).*

They are then listed in alphabetical order under each of the D.A.I.R to Win ingredients. Each key is then explained and followed by an example of a real life application and a useful proverb. This is in an effort to provide greater clarity and to reinforce the meanings to enable greater use. I have used proverbs because of my love for them, and because proverbs by their nature are wise sayings and usually survival tactics for problem-solving and success. With this kind of composition, I believe the keys are user friendly, and I hope that people of all ages will use them as needed.

Note well that the keys are not listed in a step by step order but merely captured under the D.A.I.R to Win ingredients. You can, however, organize a set of keys if you wish in a particular order to treat with an issue or when engaged in planning.

However, each key can be used individually. Therefore, feel free to draw from any of the 100 keys according to your need. Note further that some keys are similar, therefore study them carefully, because I have learnt from experience, not every key that fits a key hole turns that lock.

USEFUL DEFINITIONS

It is important before you begin using this book that you familiarize yourself with the definition of these key terms used throughout the book:

Keys to Win: These are problem-solving and success strategies which help us to live effectively and get the most out of life—personally, professionally, relationally, intellectually, emotionally, spiritually and financially. They are captured in catchy phrases to reflect the key principles, concepts or actions required to live successfully.

Win: This means to be effective, to overcome and to be successful.

W.I.N: This is an acronym which means to:

W — weather the storms of life.

I — intentionally plan for your success.

N — never give up on life and never

give up hope.

Win at Life: This term refers to living purposefully and effectively; not to be defeated by life's challenges; to achieve your goals and overcome adversities; to live the meaningful, productive and successful life you were designed to live; to live or do well in the seven key areas of life, which are reflected on the wheel of wellness for total wellness. These areas are:

1. Career/Occupational/Vocational Wellness
2. Spiritual Wellness
3. Financial Wellness
4. Physical Wellness
5. Emotional Wellness
6. Social Wellness
7. Intellectual Wellness

SECTION II: 100 LIFE-WINNING KEYS

You never get a headache from winning.
—Serbian Proverb

DECISION AND DESIGN

*Good planning and hard work lead
to prosperity, but hasty shortcuts
lead to poverty.*
—Bible Proverb

This section contains twenty-five (25) keys, proverbs and real life applications to aid you in making wise decisions and design a strategic plan or blueprint for your success.

1. Win with Accountability

Your chances of success generally improve with accountability, especially if the one holding you accountable is someone you respect or fear. The simple acts of setting deadlines and making reports or just thinking that someone will evaluate or audit your work psychologically will enable you to work more efficiently and carefully.

I notice when persons or businesses have to be audited that the systems work better. People are more careful in how they handle the company's resources. When you have to answer to someone regarding a goal or your performance, you tend to be more careful about what you do. The next time you set a goal, ask someone to hold you accountable. You can simply say to the person, I will tell you how it goes or ask the person to check on you. You will be surprised how well you will do as a result.

Accountability can keep you out of trouble and help you to perform your duties better. Set up an accountability system or get an accountability partner today.

Real Life Application: In 2011, I learnt the power of accountability after I had completed a training called *Key Concepts*, in which I was required to give a monthly report to a coach about the implementation of my action plan, which was created at the training. In that time period, I grew tremendously. In fact, the "Design to Win" course and several initiatives were birthed out of that experience. Had I just simply gone to a conference and not been held accountable, to put into practice what I would probably not have been able to produce the course, "Design to Win." My coach, Rev. Courtney Richards, in that period became my mentor and he has helped me to win at life, guiding me through perhaps the most difficult period of my life to date and taught me that I am loved, prized and valued.

Key Proverb: *God gave burden, also shoulders.* —Yiddish Proverb

2. Win with Advanced Preparation

This key is based on the 6Ps: prior proper preparation prevents poor performance. This key should not be confused with *Design to Win*, although when you use that key you are actually preparing to win.

The Roman philosopher Seneca said: "Luck is what happens when preparation meets opportunity." Preparation is making decisions to position yourself for tomorrow's opportunities. It is anticipating what is ahead and getting ready for it, be it good or bad.

This key is basic common sense, but it is often overlooked, especially by those who love to do things at the last minute. I have discovered that advanced preparation based on accurate information and clarity helps you to win. Advanced preparation does not prevent eventualities, but it forces you to anticipate what is ahead and to get ready as best as you can for the possibilities. Advanced preparation is a good time-management, business and life growth practice that should be employed in every area of your life, if you intend to win. This is one key that requires constant use.

Real Life Application: It is said that every minute spent in preparation saves you 10 minutes in execution. I practice preparing for my days, weeks and months in advance. I normally make my daily things to do list the night before which tends to help me get through my activities more quickly throughout the following day. With this habit, I don't have to wonder what to do when I get up, I just get to work because I am ready for the day. It has given me a sense of being in charge of my day so that, as author Jim Rohn says, "you run the day instead of the day running you."

When I prepare for the upcoming year at the end of the current year, I also accomplish more. I break up the year into quarters and make 100-day plans, which I further break up into monthly, weekly and then daily activities. This has greatly improved my efficiency and rate of success.

Key Proverb: *Tomorrow belongs to the people who prepare for it today.* —African Proverb

3. Win with Best Practices

This is closely aligned with *Using Templates/-Models to Win*. For example, whenever you are starting a business, engaging in a new venture or attending a new school, it is always good to find out what are the best practices and seek to follow them. Best practices are the practices that generally bring outstanding results. If you operate by best practices at home, school or work, you will win.

What are the best study practices if you are a student? Why not talk to older, successful students to find out what study techniques they used to pass their exams or which ones they would recommend? If you are a cook, then what are the best cooking techniques? Once again, why not talk to a successful chef about their techniques or research the best cooking techniques and follow them? If you are a manager, why not investigate the best management or leadership practices and follow suit? When companies or individuals follow best practices, it will help them to maintain standards of excellence because they are following what has been proven to work. Why not apply this key to every area of your life? To find out the best practices, do internet research, read books and ask others questions.

Real Life Application: My friend Dee is excellent at using this key. When she decided to become an author, she studied the self-publishing industry. She got her questions answered and employed the principles she learnt, which resulted in the production of her first book which has been doing really well. When it was time to publish my book, she guided me well based on the best practices she had learnt. Her advice was priceless and saved me from making some rather expensive mistakes.

Key Proverb: *He who does not know the road to a stream should be guided by pieces of broken clay pot.* —African Proverb

4. Win with a Burning Desire (Passion)

Success expert Napoleon Hill, who studied the success of over 500 people for 25 years, saw this as the starting point of success. All achievement begins with a burning desire. When you have passion for something, you will work harder. All high achievers engage in work they love or work that they have learnt to love.

What is it that you do that makes you excited or gives you a feeling of significance? This is an indication of your passion. What is it that you can spend hours doing effortlessly without feeling drained? This is a clue to your passion. Find out how you can use this passion to serve others. When you have a burning desire to accomplish something, you will be more disciplined in that area. In fact, discipline at this stage will seem almost natural. Having a burning desire to serve or achieve will aid in your success.

Real Life Application: Several years ago, I watched a television interview of the popular Jamaican Dancehall artiste Shaggy on Ian Boyne's *Profile*. Shaggy explained how much he loved to sing and DJ while in college and had been doing it merely as a hobby for years. Eventually his passion became his career, and he has now become a successful artiste doing what he loves. This is an example of turning your passion into profit.

Key Proverb: *Send a child where he wants to go and you will see his pace.* —African Proverb.

5. Win with Clarity

Progress is impeded when we don't have a clear sense of what we are trying to achieve or what we have been asked to do or want to do in life. Clarity is knowing or having a clear understanding of what is required. It is foundational to success. Clarity gives one confidence and can prevent losses, embarrassment and failure. Clarity decreases stress levels. Clarity prevents confusion.

This is how you gain clarity: before you begin any task, ask or research what needs to be done or what is required. If you have an essay to write, be clear on what the question is asking. If you are seeking a job, be clear on the kind of job you want. If you are being hired, be clear on what you are hired to do so that you don't waste time on the job. If you are joining an organization or being given any role, be sure to know what is expected of you. This is how you gain clarity which is a vital ingredient to win at life. In every case as much as possible seek clarity before you do anything.

Real Life Application: I was asked to do a series of teachings on Discipleship at a church for a week along with another teacher. To ensure we understood what we were required to do, we met with the church leader, asked him about his vision and his expectations, after which, we were able to draft a time-table for the week with the topics each teacher would cover. At the end of the meeting, I knew exactly what I needed to do. Our efforts to seek clarity made teaching so much easier.

Key Proverb: *Only a fool tests the depth of water with both feet.* —African Proverb

6. Win with Core Values

Many companies have core values and so should you in your personal life. A core value is a fundamental belief or principle that guides your behaviour. These help you to know what is right or wrong. These are the standards by which you live and are basically non-negotiable. They are together the lens by which you measure your decisions or organize your life, and they determine your character or are a reflection of your character.

Examples of core values are: honesty, creativity, integrity, faith, family, work, innovation, respect, peace of mind etc. Faith and peace of mind are two of my core values. You should take some time to sit and determine your core values. Perhaps you should look at a list online or the list of the core values of people you admire and then decide which of those would work for you. Make your list of 3-10 core values today.

Real Life Application: One of my core values is peace of mind. Every time I violate this core value I am miserable. On one occasion, I hired someone to work on a project, and I became very uncomfortable with the decision and the person. In fact, it did cause me some sleepless nights, because I had no peace about it. I eventually outsourced the job to someone else, and my peace of mind returned. In fact, the project turned out better than I had imagined.

Key Proverb: *Wherever a man goes to dwell, his character goes with him.* —African Proverb

7. Win with Faith

As a Christian, it is my Faith in God that keeps me going especially in tough times. In general, it is found that people of Faith—and not necessarily the Christian Faith—are more resilient and respond better in times of adversity. There are some challenges in life that will hit you for which only faith in God (A Higher Power) can sustain you. My Faith in Jesus Christ and my spiritual disciplines help me to cope with the storms of life; my faith helps me to be innovative and make wise decisions.

For example, it is usually during my times of solitude and prayer (communicating with God) that I get ideas for projects; insights and answers to problems and a feeling of peace and empowerment. I also have faith that my Faith gives me the strength to employ all the other keys, especially the challenging ones like *Self-discipline*, *Ask to Win*, *Win with Courage* and *Act to Win*. There are times when I know what to do but simply find it difficult to apply what I know. Many times I don't have the energy or motivation to do that which I know to be right and beneficial. In these moments I pray and after prayer, my desire to do that which is necessary usually returns. After prayer and exercising faith, I am able to win at life.

The second element of winning with faith is not necessarily religious. It is the belief in—and being sure of—your goal, even when you don't see it in the natural. It is a knowing that you will win without any outward proof. It is turning the invisible (your design and goal) into the visible. It is being sure of a result or an outcome without anything tangible to show and working to make it a reality. Having both in your arsenal is vital to winning at life.

Life Application: When I was writing my first book, I needed the courage to get sponsors. It was my Faith that fuelled me into action. There were times when I felt afraid to ask for funding and felt discouraged. Then I would either pray by myself or with a friend, after which I found the strength to write the letters or ask. In the end, after 64 rejections, 24 persons said "yes," and I received approximately half a million Jamaican dollars in sponsorship.

Key Proverb: *Faith is the vision of the heart.*
—American Proverb

8. Win with Life Purpose

This is similar to the key *Win with Reasons* but is somewhat different in focus. Napoleon Hill calls it having a chief definite aim in life. When we fail to understand the purpose of a thing already in existence, we tend to misuse, abuse, overlook, under-utilize and can in fact, miss the acres of diamonds right in our backyards. The success of any created thing is linked to the fulfilment of its purpose, that is, functioning according to its design and intended use to meet the need for which it was created. So it is with our lives as human beings.

I've heard noted leadership expert, John Maxwell, say that the two most important days of a person's life are: the day you were born and the day you discover why. *Win with Purpose* is about intentionally seeking to know one's purpose, being cognizant of it and living to fulfil it. This is essential for personal accountability, effectiveness, progress, significance and success.

Discovering your life purpose often requires a blend of introspection, self-questioning and praying if you are a person of faith and asking yourself what could I live or die for? What contribution do I want to make in the world? What are my gifts and passion and how could I use this to leave a mark in the world? What is that one thing that I could do that blends with my gifts that will add value and meaning to my life? What is my chief definite aim? Sometimes it is a journey of trial and error to discover your purpose, but it's worth the work.

Once you discover or verify your purpose it's a good idea to write purpose statements and strive to live by them. Here is my example: I exist to exalt God and empower people to win at life using my gifts of teaching, writing and speaking and raising up leaders to do the same. All successful people have a strong sense of purpose. Your life purpose is your reason for the journey on planet Earth. In our "Design to Win" course, we teach you how to find your purpose and create purpose statements.

Real Life Application: This story comes from Andrew Carnegie, an American industrialist and major philanthropist. It is said that Carnegie expressed early in his life that he wanted to spend the first half of his life making money and then the second half giving it all away. Carnegie did exactly as he had expressed. He had a chief definite aim in life, and he lived in a way that it was fulfilled.

Key Proverb: *Accomplishment of purpose is better than making a profit.* —African Proverb

9. Win with the Power of Decision

Tony Robbins captures it well when he says: "Decisions shape destiny." Let's use a travel analogy to understand the power and need for decisions. You will not travel from one place to another until you make the decision and select a destination. Your decisions influence your direction because only then can you make proper travel plans. In travel, decision precedes both departure and arrival.

In this regard, the advice of author Jim Rohn is noteworthy. Rohn explains that, "Making decisions can be likened to internal civil war... Whatever you do, don't camp at the fork in the road. Decide. It's far better to make a wrong decision than to not make one at all. Each of us must confront our emotional turmoil and sort out our feelings." The bottom line is that you cannot make progress without making decisions. Now learning to make wise decisions is another matter, and I think that is where other keys like *Core Values, Bounce it to Win, Learning More* and *Best Practices* will come in handy. However, in this regard, Rohn's advice is priceless:

Seek other people's advice, but don't take orders. And don't take 100% of anyone's advice. Make sure every decision you make is a product of your own conclusion. Be a student, not a disciple....

So when somebody asks me to make a decision about a situation, I don't offer a solution, I ask a question: What are our options? Give me the good, give me the bad, give me the pretty, give me the ugly, give me the impossible, give me the possible, give me the convenient, give me the inconvenient. Give me the options. All I want are options. And once I have all the options before me, then I comfortably and confidently make my decision.[1]

Remember no decision—no progress... no decision—no life change.

Real Life Application: Nancy had recently graduated from Holy Childhood High school, and her parents wanted her to pursue further studies abroad. Nancy, however, wanted to study in Jamaica and settled this firmly in her heart. Thus Nancy gathered data on colleges in Jamaica and all the reasons why studying locally would be beneficial. With this data she convinced her parents to let her study in Jamaica. Nancy then applied to three schools and got admitted to one, and now she is enrolled in a Jamaican university. Decision shapes destiny.

Key Proverb: *Idleness is ever the root of indecision.* —Latin Proverb

---

[1] Jim Rohn. http://www.azquotes.com/quote/827007 accessed November 25, 2016

10. Win with the Power of Design

This key is not to be confused with *Design to Win*. Design is used here as a noun and refers to the complete image or your completed plan of action. This key is what Stephen Covey, author of the *7 Habits of Highly Effective People,* refers to as "starting with the end in mind." It is envisioning the end, outcome, product or result before you take action or begin to work. It is the dream or vision and the architect's blueprint in high definition or 3D. If you are building a business, it is seeing in your mind how you want it to operate before you establish the structure. If you are the manager of a football league, it is seeing the structure of the football league before establishing plans to actualize it. It is the playwright seeing the end of the play before creating a plot to achieve that end.

In terms of your life, it is imagining what you would want or where you want to be 5-10 years from now; or what you wish others to say about you at your funeral or in your eulogy, and then seeking to live that out. In our "Design to Win" course, this is an essential key in creating your life design and is used in our "Design to Win" life planning activities. What does your life design look like? Where do you want to end up? What is your financial fitness design, your marriage design, your academic design, your emotional health design and your relationship design? Sit and begin to envision the design for different areas of your life today.

Real Life Application: In 2010, the President of the Jamaica Theological Seminary, Rev. Dr. Garnett Roper, outlined a vision for the expansion of the seminary which included the addition of an online programme, new degree offerings and having satellite campuses in other Caribbean islands. He shared his vision (design) with the staff and then took steps to implement his design. Since that time, at least four new degree programmes have been added; two campuses in the Eastern Caribbean and an online programme. His actions served as a vivid example to me of the power of design.

Key Proverb: *If you can envision it, you can accomplish it. If you can imagine it, you can reach the heavens.* —African Proverb

11. Win with Reasons

This particular key works well with *Win with the Power of Design*. In fact, it may precede it or could be a case of the chicken and the egg. If you are going to win, knowing the "why" is very important. Your reason is the oxygen that keeps your goals breathing in the tough times. Your reasons build resilience in tough times. These help you to persevere despite the odds. Renowned business philosopher Jim Rohn, once said, "when the why gets stronger, the how gets easier." Victor Frankl in *Man's Search for Meaning* says: "Those who have a 'why' to live can bear with almost any 'how.'"

Write down compelling reasons to work, to love, to start a family, to be financially independent, to support a cause, to finish school or whatever you are involved in, as this will help to boost your success. For example: in writing this book my reasons are:

   i. it will help me fulfil my life purpose,
  ii. it will help others to find ways to solve their problems, and
 iii. it will change lives.

When I reflect on these reasons, in times when I don't feel like completing the project, I review the reasons and I am motivated to finish it. I would encourage you to write 5-10 reasons for living, for your work or anything of value you are engaged in; put them on your phone or a small card and review them often.

Real Life Application: Former Tennessee football player Inky Johnson's reason for playing football was to improve the life of his mother and to set an example for his family and youths in his neighbourhood. This reason fuelled him to train hard, and eventually he was drafted into the football league. However, after a short stint in the league, he became badly injured and lost the use of his right arm. Inky nevertheless refused to give up, because he had reason to fight. Despite the injury, today Inky is an inspiration to many and is a successful business man and motivational speaker. His reasons helped him to be resilient.

Key Proverb: *The wine-skin has its reasons for smelling of pitch.* —Portuguese Proverb

12. Win with Results

This simple key reminds us that it is not activities that matter; it is results. When we become more results-oriented, we become more efficient users of our time and resources. Know the expected results (outcomes) before beginning a task and work towards those. It's not the busyness that counts; it's the results. Sometimes we can be busy with the wrong thing, and we end up majoring on the minor. We need to separate the vital few from the trivial many to get the right results. Focus on the outcome to win.

In teaching terms, we write objectives, what we want to achieve at the end of the lesson and then we plan the methodology to achieve those results. In sports, it is the trophy, the prize money, finishing first etc.; in school it is thinking of the career and the income it will generate. In sales it might be a specific number per day or a financial target. Focusing on the outcome is essential for success.

Real Life Application: It is not the number of years that the athlete trains for the Olympics that matters or how many heats s/he wins at the meet. It is the results that matter in the final race that really makes a difference. In fact, it is the top three positions that really count in the end—gold, silver and bronze.

Key Proverb: *The end praises the work.* — Italian Proverb

13. Win with Rewards

I find that the greater or more enticing and compelling the reward, the more effort we will exert to achieve something. Just think of talent shows like *Digicel Rising Stars*, *The Voice* and *American Idol*. It is the reward that entices persons to enter. Think of that scholarship or that sports trophy. Does it not motivate you to succeed? As Jim Rohn says, "If you know the prize, you will pay the price." When you are feeling lazy or lack motivation to do something, give yourself an enticing reward, and when you achieve it, celebrate your achievements. Some companies give their workers a bonus to motivate them to work more efficiently. Ask yourself what is the reward for any task you have been given, or wish to do. This will fuel your success.

Real Life Application: Jamaica's world famous athlete Usain Bolt is evidence of this. Usain has said on many occasions that he does not like training. However, the prize of winning and the rewards of winning compel him to do what he does not like. Today he is a success and a living track and field legend.

Key Proverb: *Reward sweetens labor.* — Dutch Proverb

14. Win with Truth

Many times we struggle emotionally because we have false beliefs about ourselves or we have been fed lies about our identity and self-worth. It is the truth about who we are that will set us free, although sometimes it may hurt. Although we are sceptical about truth in this post-modern world, the concept of truth forms the basis of our justice system and is a core element of society's operations. False assumptions or errant assumptions can also lead to false judgement and evaluations, which can in turn destroy relationships or cause us to respond or think in ways other than we should. My friend author, Ric Couchman supplied this illustration to prove the point of the latter.

> *I see my partner talking to a stranger at a party, and I observe that they both are smiling and appear very comfortable with each other. I assume that the stranger is hitting on my partner and that my partner—based on his/her reaction—seems to be enjoying it. It is a conclusion that I arrived at based on no substantive evidence. I immediately assumed some amorous intent of the stranger and never once considered other possibilities about him or her, that perhaps the stranger was a cousin, a very good friend, etc.*
>
> *If we give into assumptions without carefully testing or awaiting clarification of behaviour we might observe in others, we run the risk of giving into more suspicions and as a consequence undermine trust—the essential ingredient in a relationship.*

This is why in mediation, crisis or conflict management, knowing the truth is vital to bring about a resolution.

Real Life Application: Les Brown was told that he was "educatedly mentally retarded" and so was pushed back from a higher grade to a lower grade. This affected his outlook on life. He started to believe he was not capable of sound reasoning, and therefore would not attempt to do tasks other children would do. This behaviour did not change until a teacher, Mr. Washington, challenged him with the words: "Someone's opinion of you does not have to become your reality."

This truth transformed his life and today he is a multimillionaire, a business man, former politician and a renowned motivational speaker. He had a moment of truth that changed his life. Knowing the truth about who you are brings liberation. This is an important key to win at life.

Key Proverb: *A lie runs until it is overtaken by the truth.* —Cuban Proverb

15. Accept the Inevitable to Win

There are some things in life that are inevitable, and yet when they come, we are caught off guard. This ought not to be. Knowing the inevitable should remove some of the sting out of the situation and make us better prepared. I find knowing that some things are bound to happen does help to reduce the pain.

When you learn to accept the things that cannot be changed, it eases your mental stress. It helps you to be less disappointed and respond better to that situation, because the surprise or strangeness has been removed from it. As we learn basic human behaviour and psychology, we are better equipped to deal with the situations.

For example, death is often painful but sure to happen. However, we don't know when it will occur, and yet many persons do not take out any life insurance. Many persons would rather not think about it. Sickness is another example of one of life's "inevitables," and yet some persons do not make any provisions for it. In our Jamaican High School, the Caribbean Council Examinations is another inevitable in the fourth or fifth form, and yet many parents are caught unprepared and do their children a disservice. Despite five years of notice, they fail to save any money to pay for the subjects for their children. Even as a child, you can begin saving or seeking sponsorship early, so that if your life is spared, and your parents do not prepare, you can still sit your exams. This key when applied will help us to minimize or prevent damage.

Real Life Application: When Sandy began caring for her dad, he had been diagnosed with cancer. Thus Sandy prepared for the inevitable. Many people expected him to live for only a few months, but he lived for six years. During that time, Sandy made preparations for his health care and for his eventual death. When her father died, Sandy, though hurt and grieved, had no difficulties planning for the funeral or getting a death certificate. She was able to have the funeral within two weeks, and there was no financial burden to anyone. This is the power of accepting the inevitable things of life.

Key Proverb: *When a chick ignores its mother's warning, the eagle grasps it for a meal.* —African Proverb

16. Design to Win

The *Design to Win* process is extensive and is explored in detail in our course and the textbook bearing the same name. This key is paired with *"Win with the Power of a Design,"* however; it takes it one step further. Many people as children had a vision of where they wanted to go in life. They dreamt of doing one thing or the other but never pursued it. *Design to Win* is about intentionally planning or strategizing for your success. Winning is not accidental. One of the saddest things in life is to end up at an unintended destination and then ask yourself in despair, "how did I get here?" It was a challenge from Jim Rohn that opened my eyes to the importance of this key. I will share his challenge with you. May his challenge open your eyes to the need to *Design to Win.*

Here is a good question to ask yourself: Ten years from now you will surely arrive. The question is, where...? In 10 years, we'll arrive at an either well de-

signed destination or an un-designed destination... We don't want to kid ourselves about where; we don't want to kid ourselves about the road we're walking... Now's the time to fix the next 10 years... Here's what we don't want to engage in: disillusion; hoping without acting; wishing without doing. The key is to take a look and say, "Where am I? What could I do to make the changes will make sure that I can take more certain daily steps toward the treasure I want, the mental treasure, the personal treasure, the spiritual treasure, the financial treasure?[2]

When we design to win, we not only see the image or desire (goal), but we work out the steps to achieve the desired outcome. When we design to win, we employ several keys such as *Goal Setting, Thinking Long Term, Relationships and Resources* as well as *Accountability.* Now, this does not mean it will all go as planned, but it is better to have a plan than no plan at all, if we intend to be effective in life. We have all heard that wise saying: *If you fail to plan, then you plan to fail.*

We need a game plan for work, our finances, our relationships, our retirement and our overall health and well-being. Chances are, without one, we will end up at an unintended destination in these areas. No sports team plays without a strategy and expects to win. Practice being purposeful and intentional in all your endeavours, and you will win at life.

[2] Jim Rohn. Success Magazine. http://www.success.com/-article/rohn-where-do-you-see-yourself-in-10-years - accessed November 25, 2016.

Real Life Application: In 2014, I took four months to review and reinvent my life and engaged in a process of designing to win professionally and socially. I spent several days writing out a vision for my life and the strategies I would employ to make that vision a reality. In my design, I said I would become a personal development coach, would publish a book each year and create a personal development course called "Design to Win."

In March 2015, the first book was published and the second in April 2016. By September 2015, I had my first contract as a personal development coach delivering my "Design to Win" course to a group of eight (8) young men. This is just one of many examples of the power of this key in my life.

Key Proverb: *Strategy is better than strength.* —African Proverb

17. Imagine Big to Win

This is closely aligned to the key: *Win with the Power of Design*. It is allowing yourself to see great possibilities beyond your present realities, capacity and limitations. For example, don't just see yourself as a singer in Jamaica; see yourself performing around the world. Don't just see yourself with one business; see yourself like KFC with franchises around the world.

If you imagine small, the results might be very limited. However, if you imagine really big, even if things do not work as planned, you will still have some substantial achievement. It's as Les Brown says, "some people fail in life not because they aimed too high and missed, but they aimed too low and hit." It is imagining at such a level that it stretches your present capacity. It is being awakened to the great potential that lies in all of us and giving ourselves the right to dream big. Noted missionary William Carey put it this way: "Expect great things from God and attempt great things for God." Successful people are big thinkers. Note carefully that the level of your success is limited only by the height of your imagination. Imagine big if you want to win at life.

Real Life Application: Comedian Steve Harvey has told his story multiple times that as a child he told his teacher about his dream of being on television. At the time, Steve Harvey was ridiculed because no one from his school, his family or neighbourhood had ever accomplished that feat, and besides, Steve was a stutterer back then. His father through it all encouraged him to keep his big dream in sight, and today, Steve Harvey is a renowned TV personality who has his own television show. Don't be afraid to imagine big.

Key Proverb: *A small shrub may grow into a tree.* —African Proverb

18. Pen it to Win

This closely follows the *Design to Win* key. It is based on the observation that successful people think on paper. In fact, success expert Brian Tracy says your chances of success increase by 10x when you put your goals on paper with a plan to achieve them. Every architect records his blueprint, every designer has a sketch captured somewhere. Goals and plans that are merely in your head will not enable you to progress as well as you can. Your chances of success increase when you write the plan and make it clear.

My pastor, Rev. Rennard White often says, "that which is not written does not exist." Some persons do not keep their word or remember what they tell you, and by recording what is said, you will save yourself some trouble or embarrassment. *Pen it to Win* is more than just documenting your plans but is a good way to preserve ideas and to hold others accountable. This is the reason for books, written contracts, business plans, labels, instructions and street signs, etc.

When in meetings, record what is said then proceed to do your work with clarity. Many ideas that could perhaps result in millions of dollars have been lost because they were not recorded. As Jim Rohn says, "Your head was never meant to be a filing cabinet." In fact, my friend Sheril Morgan's mom says, "The shortest pencil is better than the longest memory," so *Pen it to Win* today.

Real Life Application: In frustration, Lisa told me of an experience with her Boss. After a meeting with management, her Boss had told her to work on a particular project and, having completed the project and submitted the results, her Boss denied having given her the permission to proceed. I told Lisa, "next time *pen it to win;* either you take notes or email him after each meeting to verify what is your assignment."

To Lisa's credit, she found a way to employ the key to her success. She asked her Boss to send her emails regarding the tasks he requires of her. He has complied and since then things have been going smoothly. She used *pen it to win* to work in her favour.

Key Proverb: *The faintest ink is more powerful than the strongest memory.* —Chinese Proverb

19. Set Smart Goals to Win

Success expert, Brian Tracy, often says: "Success is goals and all else is complementary." Successful people set goals in writing for their future and make plans to achieve them. When we set goals, these ought to be smart and compelling goals. A smart and compelling goal is one that is specific, clearly written with the end in mind, and backed by strong reasons for its accomplishment in a given time period. They afford clarity for decision-making, peace of mind, having clearer focus, efficient time-management, and enable you to live purposefully. Additionally, if you are working on a group initiative or project, setting goals helps you to explain to others what you are trying to accomplish, and therefore what they need to do to contribute and support your initiative.

Real Life Application: In 1979, interviewers asked new graduates from the Harvard MBA Program about their goals and found that:

- 84% had no specific goals at all;

- 13% had goals but they were not committed to paper;

- 3% had clear, written goals and plans to accomplish them;

In 1989, the interviewers again interviewed the graduates of that class. Here are the results 10 years later:

- The 13% of the class who had goals were earning, on average, twice as much as the 84 percent who had no goals at all.

- Even more staggering—the three percent who had clear, written goals were earning, on average, ten times as much as the other 97 percent put together.[3]

Let's all practise setting goals to increase our chances of success.

Key Proverb: *Before you can score, you must first have a goal.* —Greek Proverb

---

[3] Mark McCormack. *What They Don't Teach You in the Harvard Business School.1986*

20. Think to Win

The concept here is to actually spend time generating ideas and engaging in problem solving, reflection and creative thinking. The idea here is to intentionally sit and think in solitude and generate ideas to solve problems or to engage a group in the thinking process through brainstorming. One can practice this everyday or five days a week or every quarter. In fact, personal development expert Earl Nightingale encouraged people to generate 20 ideas each day, five days a week. He says this will revolutionize your life. Most of the ideas may be foolish but you only need one good idea to make a difference. Taking the time to think is important especially when you are leading others. It will help you take stock of your business.

Brian Tracy encourages us to use this thinking technique to solve problems. He says we should turn the problem into a question and ask how it can be solved and then write down our answers. For example, in one of his YouTube videos he explains that if you are having financial challenges you should ask: "How can I earn more money to meet X need? How can I earn $X in a year? Then write down all 20 answers that come to mind. The first 5 will be easy and the last 5 will be the hardest but stick with it." This strategy has worked for me many times.

Real Life Application: In 2014, one of my mentees, who was then in 4th form, employed this thinking strategy and wrote down 20 ways in which she could get a new laptop for the summer. As a group, we helped her with the ideas, and at the end of the summer, two of the ideas bore fruit. Thus she was able to gather the funds to purchase a new laptop. Thinking to win really works!

Key Proverb: *Every head must do its own thing.* —African Proverb

21. Think Extreme Scenarios to Win

This key should be used with its cousins *Design to Win*, *Win with Proper Preparation* and *Think Long Term to Win*. When you are faced with a challenge or contemplating a situation, ask yourself these two questions:

1. What is the worst thing that can happen?
2. What is the best thing that can happen?

Then ask yourself a third question: Can I handle it? Or do I have what it takes to deal with it? Whatever your response, make plans to deal with it. A best-case scenario is actually getting what you desire or more than you desired. It's a situation working in your favour. For example:

A Best-Case Scenario: If you get that scholarship to the USA, what's next? Do you have money for the visa? Are you ready to leave family and friends? If you get the job, do you have work clothes? Are you prepared to deal with the job demands? What are the job requirements?

A Worst-Case Scenario: If my mother dies, how will I manage? If I am evicted, where will I go? If we get a category five hurricane, what would I need to survive? Think of the answers and put a plan in place to mitigate against these adverse situations or to deal with the effects of the best-case scenarios. This technique will relieve stress and worry and help you win in every area of your life. Of course there are things that will happen that you never plan for but this technique will help you live more effectively.

Real Life Application: Sandra has been wondering if she should leave her job and apply for a position she saw advertised in another company. Sandra asked for my advice, and I told Sandra to think of the best-case and worst-case scenario and make her decision. What if you do not apply? What do you have to lose by applying, and if your application is successful, what is your exit strategy?

With this in mind, Sandra applied for the new post and has begun to set her office in order, in case her application is successful. If her application is unsuccessful, she still has a job. It's a clear win-win situation with this kind of thinking.

Key Proverb: *Don't throw away your nets, if you catch nothing; you never know what the gods are planning next.* —African Proverb

22. Think Bite Sizes to Win

When you have a task to do that seems very large or overwhelming, breaking it up into smaller pieces will decrease your stress and anxiety levels. When you have a huge target or a project, breaking it up in bite size pieces will help you to put it all together. Regarding a project here is what works. List everything that needs to be done, put the tasks in order of priority and then begin doing them one task at a time, or you can delegate or outsource things on the list. Listing the component parts will show you what to delegate and makes working as a team easier. If it's a course assignment, first make an outline and then write topic by topic. It works with achieving your dreams and goals. It works with getting through the week or the year.

All you need to do is list everything you can think of that is needed and work at it day by day, especially when you feel overwhelmed. Concentrate on what is needed at this moment and work moment by moment. In the end it will all add up. Don't try to do everything all at once. "By the yard it's hard but inch by inch it's a cinch."

For example, suppose you have a million dollars to raise. You could think of 1000 people giving $1000.00. If you have a book to write, write one page a day. If you have 10 assignments, don't try to do them all at once; do them in portions. If you have a whole book to read, read it a little at a time and eventually you will finish. Focus on the big picture (the outcome), but work on it piece by piece.

Real Life Application: I have applied this concept to finish writing this book. I gave myself weekly writing targets of 4500 words or writing 10 keys at a time and thus was able to complete the keys. Breaking up the task in portions really contributes to completing the whole.

Key Proverb: *The best way to eat an elephant in your path is cut him up into little pieces.* —African Proverb

23. Think Long Term to Win

Successful people are long-term thinkers. When we think about the future in 5-10 year blocks or even eternity, we tend to make wiser decisions. I find this is easiest to understand financially. For example, a US$50 annual credit card user fee over 10 years will be US$500. Now imagine 10,000 people paying that small fee annually! Over time, this is quite a huge sum of money collected in user fees. What if you saved that sum for 10 years, or invested that money in a mutual fund or some growth fund? You would reap the benefits over time. The banks are masters at thinking and profiting from long-term thinking.

The small fees do add up over time. It is the same with your monthly web-hosting fees, utility bills, and your daily habits, etc. They all add up and you may not like the results in hindsight. When you make decisions today, think of the long-term implications. For example, do you think the person you are fond of will be a good husband, father, wife or mother for the future? Is your current course of study in line with your long-term goals? Are your current spending habits in line with your long-term financial goals? Are your eating habits in line with your long-term health goals? Are your daily activities in line with your long-term goals? Do you have long-term goals? Everything you do is leading somewhere. Will you like the destination based on your current activities? *Think long-term to win.*

Real Life Application: Tony as a young adult began preparing for retirement early. He employed the power of long-term thinking and wanted to become financially independent and retire early. Tony accomplished this feat and was able to retire in his 40s. Tony thought long-term and made wise financial decisions early in his life. He has accomplished a feat most people have not at his age.

Key Proverb: *A nuh wan day monkey waan wife.* (Translation: It is not for a day that a monkey wants a wife.) —Jamaican Proverb

24. Think Succession and Legacy to Win

If you are not around, is there someone else who can do your job, run your business or organization? Is what you are doing only for the present? When you start a business or organization, you need to think in these terms. When you have a family, you should also think in these terms. What are the things that are worth passing on or sustaining? Who can manage when you are not around?

In leadership terms, if there is no successor, the leader has failed. In family terms, a wise parent leaves an inheritance for his grandchildren. This is why it is important to not just have followers but to develop leaders. Author John Maxwell has a book by that very name, *Developing the Leaders Around You*. Investing in leadership development is the best way to ensure your legacy lives on. Succession planning and leadership development go hand in hand. In terms of legacy, we should be concerned about building things to last a long time. What family practices, traditions, principles, etc. do you want to outlive you? I want to encourage you to develop a plan and find a way to pass it on to others and ensure that you bear fruit in life that will last.

Real Life Application: Before I left my post in my previous career with Operation Mobilization, I prepared someone to function in my post. I also created a procedural manual as a guide to help those who would serve in subsequent years. Documenting things is an excellent way to preserve one's legacy or provide a template for others to function. Thankfully, two years later, this person continues to function in said post, and the work of the agency in Jamaica continues.

Key Proverbs: *When a mighty tree falls, the birds are scattered into the bush.* —African Proverb

25. Use Templates and Models to Win

While this is similar to the key *Win with Best Practices*, it is somewhat different. The template does not have to be the best. People, animals, processes, situations and things can be used as models and templates to guide you in solving your problem. When you have been given a task and are uncertain how to approach it, find a template, that is, something similar to be used as a guide. There is no need to re-invent the wheel. You can modify the template to meet your need. The Microsoft Publisher programme is built on this concept.

However, this key applies to every area of life to make things easier. For example: If I do not know how to price an item, all I need to do is to find something similar, check the price and use that to price my item. If I am writing an essay on a topic, I can get a copy of a similar essay and use that as a guide. The same can be done in writing letters, making business decisions and solving everyday problems.

If you have a personal problem, find those who have overcome it successfully and use them as a template. This is why stories and testimonies inspire us. The sharing provides insight to solve our own problems and the sharers become the template.

Real Life Application: Recently my colleague asked me to prepare the programme for our annual Job Fair. In order to do this, I simply went to Microsoft Publisher, selected a template of a programme and adapted it to my purpose. This is the power of working with a model. The programme design turned out to be quite beautiful because of the model I used.

Key Proverb: *A sculptor that does not know how to make a gong should look at the kite's tail.* —African Proverb

ATTITUDES AND ACTIONS

He who wants to eat honey should endure the stings.
—Lebanese Proverb

This section outlines forty-three (43) actions, skills and habits which you should learn and adopt along your life journey to win at life. There are also forty-three (43) proverbs and real life applications to further fuel your success.

26. Win with Courage

Author, Mark Twain says: "Courage is not the absence of fear. It is acting in spite of it." When you have been knocked down by life, it will take courage to get back up. It will take courage to act on your dreams when no one believes in you. It will take courage to face your fears, whatever they might be, if you intend to conquer them. It will take courage to go after a dream with no money and to ask for funding. It takes courage to leave your comfort zone, which is the only way to grow. It will take courage to forgive after being hurt. This will perhaps be your biggest test if you intend to win at life but more on that later when we get to that key.

Courage is like a muscle that must be exercised. The more you use it, the better it develops. It is a discipline that gets better with practice. It is as my friend Shauna-Gay Gregory-Edwards writes: "running towards the roar."

A good way to build your courage is to have strong reasons to act. For example, if you need courage to raise funds for a cause and you are afraid to ask for money, write down all the reasons why the cause is important and what may happen if your organization no longer exists. If it's a cancer cause, think of the people who will benefit and then arm yourself to act. When the reason to act is bigger than yourself and is tied to others and not just your personal benefit, this builds courage.

One of the benefits of exercising courage is the increase in self-esteem and confidence. There are many treasures to be received when you begin to act courageously. In what way do you need to exercise courage to win today? What treasures are eluding you because you will not exercise courage?

Real Life Application: It was almost one month before the launch of my second book, and I still had not acquired the funds to print the book. Armed with courage, I wrote to a particular printery and asked for a meeting with the CEO. The response to my email came suddenly, and I was told to meet with someone else in his stead. It was someone I had never met before but armed with courage and prayer, I made my presentation and I was marvellously surprised. I gained favour and was able to secure a printing deal, and thus my book was printed in time for the launch. Indeed fortune favours the bold!

Key Proverb: *Fortune favours the bold.* — Latin Proverb

27. Win with the Golden Rule

This is the principle of doing unto others what you would have done to you. It is a law of reciprocity; the principle of treating others as one would wish to be treated. It exists across all cultures, and if practised, ensures you win at life.

John Maxwell has written a book entitled, *There Is No Such Thing As Business Ethics*, based on this one key. This key is crucial in building business and life. The Golden Rule is the basis of ethics across many cultures. It can also be stated in the negative as Confucius wrote: "Do not do to others what you do not want them to do to you."

For example, what if before you told someone something hurtful, you were to say to yourself, *what if I were told these words, how would I feel?* If the golden rule were followed, crime and injustice would be eliminated. In a personal way, the golden rule helps us to empathize and exercise self-control and maintain order. Are you living by the Golden Rule?

Real Life Application: A young man came to me in need of desperate financial assistance. His case was genuine but I had limited funds. Initially, I told him I could not help and then I remembered the many times I received help when I was in a position similar to his. I therefore made the sacrifice and assisted him because I was able to empathize. Interestingly, the next day I received a cheque that I had not expected at that particular time. This was an added bonus for going the extra mile prompted by the Golden Rule.

Key Proverb: *Consideration is the parent of wisdom.* —Latin Proverb

28. Win with Gratitude

Many studies extol the virtues of gratitude. In fact, it is scientifically proven that this key has great benefits. According to Amy Morin in *Forbes Magazine*, "grateful people experience fewer aches and pains and they report feeling healthier than other people, according to a 2012 study published in *Personality and Individual Differences*.[4]"

I have often found that when I am feeling discouraged once I begin to express gratitude for what I have instead of focusing on what I don't have, I immediately begin to feel better even if my situation does not change. Gratitude can be expressed audibly or in written

---

[4] Amy Morin. Forbes Magazine. *Personality Difference.* November 2014.

form to someone else or to one's self. Some people (including me) keep a gratitude journal. Expressing gratitude is one of my daily success habits; indeed, I am very thankful that I express gratitude regularly. Why not try it today?

Real Life Application: In June 2014, I remember feeling quite sad and distressed about my financial predicament, and in my angst, I remembered the power of gratitude. Thus, I began to sing a song about the things I was blessed with: roof up above me, place, to sleep, shoes on my feet and food on my table. As I sang, I began to feel a sense of relief and gradually my fears were allayed. I have found ever so often that gratitude is an antidote to discouragement, and I now use it daily.

Key Proverb: *Loose teeth are better than no teeth.* —African Proverb

29. Win with Hope for the Future

I love what Bishop Desmond Tutu, Nobel Peace Prize Laureate, says about hope: "Hope is being able to see that there is light despite all of the darkness." The compilation of all these keys is an expression of hope, that no matter how dark the days and the experience, light will come somehow, someday. The opposite of hope is despair and despair does nothing to enhance anyone's life. Despair kills and that is why it is important to have hope for the future, if we want to win at life. Hope is that confident expectation or that glimmer of positive expectation that you can overcome; that something good awaits you in the future, no matter how bleak it looks now.

One way of stimulating hope in hard times is to find models of triumph and success. It is to find stories of those who have conquered great adversities. Their stories will encourage you to not give up. Having hope for the future is foundational to living with passion and fervour. It is vital to achieve everything of value. The road to success will be tough. Every dream will be tested and it is the hope of fulfilment that lights the way. Therefore, I wish for you to become a prisoner of hope. It will truly help you to win at life.

Real Life Application: I often use successful people and those who defy the odds as models of hope. I say to myself, "If they did it so can I." For example, I have several female friends who married after the age of 40. Their examples give me hope on the days I feel sad about my status as an unmarried woman in my mid-thirties. I reflect on them and I feel inspired. Thus, despair is kept at bay and hope springs eternal.

Key Proverb: *He who has health has hope; and he who has hope, has everything.* — Arab Proverb

30. Win with a Positive Attitude

Renowned Motivational Speaker, Zig Ziglar says, "It's your attitude not your aptitude that determines your altitude." More people are fired from their jobs not because they lack the skill but because of poor attitudes. More students get in trouble because of their attitudes rather than their aptitudes. Your attitude is your way of thinking or feeling that manifests in a particular behaviour. I'll speak to negativity to help us see the value of a positive attitude.

Negative thinking often results in negative behaviours. Negative thinking very often says "I can't do this or that" before even attempting to do it. It is seeing a problem in every solution. It is always looking on the negative side of things and being pessimistic. It is having self-limiting beliefs. Negative thinking does not enhance your life and is not to be confused with realistic thinking. A realist does not have to be negative. Realists see things as they are.

Cultivating a positive attitude does not mean ignoring reality; it is seeing good things as they are and also better than they could be, not worse than they are. This is a concept I learnt from renowned life coach, Tony Robbins. This kind of thinking naturally leads to a positive attitude, which is an "I can" mentality. It is seeing the benefits and the brighter side of things. It is expecting something good, and this attitude enables you to perform better. Don't go through life looking for a problem in every solution. That kind of negative attitude will hinder your progress and make you difficult to work and live with.

Truly successful people generally tend to have a positive outlook on life. In most cases, this does not come naturally and therefore will demand work to develop this skill. Developing a positive attitude is a learnable skill that comes through practice. It comes with practising gratitude and actively looking for the benefit in every situation. It comes with meditating on the true, the good, the noble, the lovely and the praiseworthy (Philippians 4:8). It comes with daily doses of the inspirational. It comes with staying away from negative people or limiting your time with them. These are just some of the ways to develop and use this key.

Real Life Application: The story of Thomas Edison, who created the incandescent light bulb, is one of perseverance and a positive attitude. He refused to give up his goal, and on the 10,000th attempt was successful. When asked how he felt about the 9,999 failures, he said: "These were not failures but 9,999 ways he discovered that did not work." Now, that's the power of a positive attitude.

Key Proverb: *Anyone who is among the living has hope—even a live dog is better off than a dead lion!* —Bible Proverb

31. Win with Personal Responsibility

Popular Jamaican Dancehall artiste, Shaggy, years ago penned a song called, "It Wasn't Me." In that song, he was cheating on his partner, and yet when caught said he was not the culprit. Many of us live our lives this way. We refuse to take responsibility for our actions and our future. We either say "it's not my fault" or "it was not me." We need to take charge of our lives and give up blame to win.

Many of us have been hindered by hurts from the past, especially parental pain from childhood or abuse. In these cases we can only take responsibility for our response to the hurt. Will you let that hurt hinder you or will you let it go and move on? If you refuse to let go of the hurt, those circumstances will continue to master you. If you are going to progress, you need to take steps to be healed and move forward, even if the offender never apologizes or pays for the wrong done. This will require courage and forgiveness.

My favourite personal development E-mentor, Jim Rohn, sums it up well: "For things to change, you have to change. If you don't like things the way things are change them. You are not a tree." This means that even if we cannot change the physical circumstances we change our response and attitude. Learn to take initiative and stop waiting for people to look after your well-being. Most people are wrapped up in their own lives and concerns. They don't have much planned for you.

Therefore, you must take charge of your well-being. If you are overweight because you love food, stop saying you are "big boned"; take charge of your eating. If you are in debt, take charge of your spending habits and do the hard work to stop the cycle. If your salary is small, stop blaming the company or government; go improve your skills and value, so you can get a better job and salary. If you did something wrong, own it and move on.

You cannot change the past but you can have a say in what happens next. You can learn to do better. Even if you are not responsible for events, you are responsible for your response. Learn to give up blame and take charge of your future.

Real Life Application: My mother at an early age exercised personal responsibility for her life and refused to blame others for her mistakes. On becoming a teenage mother, she never blamed her parents or others for her struggles. She simply made a decision to uplift herself and increase her value by working and attending school while taking care of her children. Today, her life is better because she took the initiative to make it better and refused to play the blame game. She made the fulfilment of her dream her personal responsibility.

Key Proverb: *Every tub must sit on its own bottom.* —English Proverb

32. Win with Success Habits

"We become what we repeatedly do," according to Sean Covey, author of the *7 Habits of Highly Effective Teens*. Covey accurately sums up what this key is about. A habit is what we repeatedly do and what we repeatedly do daily eventually tells the tale of our lives. According to Charles Duhigg in the *Power of Habit*, habits are formed as a result of cues, routines and rewards. Habits shape our character and destiny. Both successful and unsuccessful people have habits. The idea is to find out what are the habits of successful people and adopt them as well as avoiding the habits of unsuccessful people in order to win at life. In our

"Design to Win" course, we usually have a 21-day Success Habits Challenge where we encourage participants to practice 3-5 habits over 21 days that are vital to their success. Some of the habits of successful people include: daily reading or listening to inspirational or instructional material; daily exercise; rising early; saving and expressing gratitude.

John Maxwell helps us to understand the power of habits with his Rule of Five (5). In one of his presentations, Maxwell asks: "What if I use an axe to chop a tree just five times a day, will the tree eventually fall?" Of course it will eventually fall! In the same way, the Rule of 5 is simply a series of activities that you do *every day* that are fundamental to your success. For John, his Rule of 5 are as follows: *Every day he reads, every day he files, every day he thinks, every day he asks questions* and *every day he writes*[5]. May you find your rule of 5 habits that will help you win at life!

Real Life Application: Every day I feed my mind, engage in planning, rise early, pray and express gratitude. These habits have dramatically changed my life over the last six years. The daily planning and feeding of my mind have been instrumental in providing data for speeches and writing, as well as giving useful information to help others solve their problems.

Key Proverb: *Good habits result from resisting temptation.* —Portuguese Proverb

---

[5] John Maxwell. Rule of 5. http://www.johnmaxwell.-com/blog/the-rule-of-5-for-the-john-maxwell-company

33. Win with the Power of Perspective

Have you ever had an insight that caused you to break a bad habit or that caused your life to go in an entirely new direction? That's a mind-shift or a change in perspective and interpretation. It is a breakthrough caused by a change of thought or pattern in thinking. Thinking is closely related to behaviour and often times we are trapped by negative behaviours because of our mindsets or our perspective on life. It's not what happens but our interpretation of things that happen to us that makes us emotionally well or unwell. Success expert, Jack Canfield, reminds us that events plus response equals outcome.

We all know persons who have been through great adversities, and yet they were not broken. Some of the world famous ones are for example, Nelson Mandela (South Africa) and Marcus Garvey (Jamaica). There are many more persons that we can think of, and some I am sure, are in your circles of influence. When we intentionally seek to interpret things that happen in a way that make them work in our favour, we are using the power of perspective. No wonder John Maxwell says: "Life is 10% what happens to us and 90% how we respond." It's time to use the power of perspective to win at life.

Real Life Application: During the long dark night of my soul after my second broken engagement, I remembered a quote from William Barclay that shifted me from the perspective of a victim to becoming a victor. William Barclay says: "Endurance is not just the ability to bear a hard thing, but to turn it into glory." Instead of feeling sorry for myself I sought to turn my experience into something that would be of help to others and find a way to build up myself. That perspective caused me to become what Carl Jung calls a wounded healer. This is part of what gave rise to Extra MILE Initiatives and even the publishing of these keys to win at life.

Key Proverb: *For as he thinks in his heart, so is he.* —Bible Proverb

34. Win with Resilience

Jamaican singer, Prince Buster has a song entitled, "Hard Man Fi Dead." In that song, the first line of the chorus says: "You pick him, you lick (hit) him dung (down), him bounce right back. What a hard man fi (to) dead." This is the essence of resilience and the heart of winning at life. You have to resolve that you will be like a cat with nine lives. You refuse to die. You will not give up no matter how bad it is or how bad it gets. Resilience means you bounce back by striving for your goal no matter what. On your life journey there will be many hits but don't stay down... knocked down but not knocked out. If you stay down, you lose the fight. Resilience is a skill that can be learnt through practice. It can be developed by building strong ties, having care and support, high expectations for success, opportunities for meaningful participation, establishing clear and consistent boundaries and by learning valuable life skills and strategies. The keys given in this book are all aimed at helping you to develop resilience.

Real Life Application: Les Brown in his video: *It's Not Over Until I Win*, tells the story of how he had to ask multiple times before he landed a job at radio station. His teacher, Mr. Leroy Washington, encouraged him to continue trying. Mr. Washington told him that most people are so negative in life, that they have to say no seven times before they say yes. After being rejected repeatedly by the same persons, Les was eventually hired because of his persistence and his ability to bounce back from rejection. Eventually Les became a great disc jockey at the same radio station.

Key Proverb: *Fall down seven times and stand up eight.* —Japanese Proverb

35. Win with Self-Discipline

In the *Miracle of Self Discipline,* Brian Tracy explains that self-discipline is the power to make yourself do what you ought to do, whether you feel like it or not. This, he explains, is the master key to success. Self-discipline is learning to master our feelings and emotions. It is the ability to sacrifice the immediate and temporary for that which is lasting and more rewarding. It is learning to pay the price. It is learning to delay pleasure for future gain.

Jamaica's fastest runner over 100m is the legendary Usain Bolt, and he has taught me much about the power and need for self-discipline. Usain dislikes training but for the prize of being the best in his field, he will set aside his dislike for training and do the gruelling training in order to win. In the documentary, *The Fastest Man Alive*, we see that the training is so gruelling that his father cannot bear to watch him train. Sometimes Usain even vomits. His regime includes training 1½ hours three times each week. Without the habit of doing what is necessary instead of doing what feels good, Usain would not be the successful athlete he is today.

One of the particular benefits of self-discipline that I love, is the fact that when we exercise self-discipline, our confidence and self-esteem rise. We definitely feel better about ourselves. Therefore let me ask you: are you willing to deny yourself and delay gratification to reap lasting rewards, or will you let your feelings master you?

Real Life Application: As taken from the explanation, Usain Bolt trains at least three times each week for one and half hours in preparation for athletic competition, although he dislikes training. That discipline has paid off, and today he is a legendary Jamaican sprinter, the fastest 100m athlete in the world.

Key Proverb: *He that would eat the fruit, must climb the tree.* —Scottish Proverb

36. Act to Win

Thinking alone will not guarantee success. Planning or designing by itself will not guarantee success. Action is the master key to success. As long as you have the seed in your hand it will never become a tree until it is planted. Good intentions alone do not guarantee success. Someone once said that the road to hell is paved with good intentions. Knowledge alone does not bring change until it is acted upon. It's not what you know; it's what you apply that makes the difference.

Real Life Application: In early 2015, I conceived the idea of an empowerment event and for months I did nothing about it. However, towards the end of 2015, I made it a goal to actualize the event in 2016, even though I had no funds to execute. I then gathered a team together and with faith, frugality and ingenuity, the event *Behind TheSmile* was executed in February 2016. I acted to win.

Key Proverb: *A roaring lion kills no game.* — African Proverb

37. Adjust Your Expectations to Win

This speaks to changing our mindset when we are unhappy or feeling upset in certain situations. Our unhappiness is usually caused by unmet expectations, and as such, if our expectations change, our feelings are also likely to change. I have found this to be quite true—

when we change our expectations, everything changes.

If a truck is built to carry 500 tonnes, don't be upset if it breaks down when you put 1000 tonnes on it. When we change our expectations of situations or individuals, we often find release and are better able to deal with them. Perhaps your expectations are too high and, as long as you don't change them, you will continue to be disappointed when others do not measure up. In what situation will you apply this key today?

Real Life Application: Jean was very disappointed with her boss's behaviour and had become quite angry with him. This caused a strain on their relationship and a strain on Jean's emotional state. I told Jean to adjust her expectations of her boss and to change how she responded to him. Over the next couple of months, I noticed that Jean complained less, as she was less surprised by her boss's behaviour. Jean's perspective changed, and so did her stress levels.

Key Proverb: *When the music changes, so does the dance.* —African Proverb

38. Ask to Win

The courage to ask is essential to success. Jesus said: "Ask and it shall be given" (Matthew 7:7). His brother James said: "You have not because you ask not" (James 4:3). Do you realize how many things you actually have because you asked? Have you considered how many things you do not have or know because you did not ask? At the root of the resistance to ask is the fear of rejection or appearing foolish. But if you never ask, the possibility of not receiving is 100%. If you ask, your chance of receiving goes up by 50%.

Learn to ask for what you need. Ask intelligently and repeatedly. Ask with the attitude of a child, says Jim Rohn. When children ask, they expect to receive, and they will often nag you until they get what they want. Ask persistently, if it is something you really desire. We should emulate this attitude of theirs.

In this regard, Jack Canfield and Mark Victor Hansen in *The Aladdin Factor* give a formula to encourage persistence noting that it is a numbers game. It's called the SW formula: "Some will, some won't, so what, someone's waiting." I find that asking for help is humbling but necessary to win at life. Remember Canfield's SW formula, the next time you go asking for something. Ask for something today!

Real Life Application: In 2016, I had a desire to develop a long-term partnership with the Women's Center of Jamaica Foundation. I thought about offering along with my books my "Design to Win" personal development course to the teenage mothers to empower them to win at life. I therefore called the Director, expressed my interest and asked permission to do so. She encouraged me to send a proposal in writing. The proposal was accepted and in January 2017, I began my first set of "Design to Win" workshops with a group of young mothers at the center.

The courage to ask has opened a marvellous door to impact young lives positively.

Key Proverb: *Ask paas yu cyaanh laas pass.* (Translation: Ask the way (path) and you will not lose the way.) —Jamaican Proverb

39. Be Adaptable and Flexible to Win

This speaks of openness to change and changing. I'm sure you have heard the phrase: *When in Rome do as the Romans do.* We have to be willing to change gears, if we want to win. We are in a rapidly changing environment. Look at the revolution in the electronics industry and the telecommunications industry. The way we communicate has dramatically changed in the last 15 years. I remember when we had to line up at a phone booth to make a call. Now we have smart phones that take pictures and videos. Now we can video chat. We don't need a camera and a phone as separate devices. One instrument can do both things. Businesses that do not keep up will go under.

In life, many times things will not go as planned, because we don't know the future. Sometimes our best plan is faulty, because we don't have all knowledge. Sometimes what we have planned is not what is best for us, and therefore, we have to be open to change. Our way is not always the right way. Organizations have to change to remain relevant. However, our core values should remain unchanging. We have to learn to be flexible and adaptable in order to win at life.

Real Life Application: In 2010, the Jamaica Theological Seminary made a decision to become more flexible with its course offerings and to follow the trend towards online learning. Today, the seminary has a thriving online learning programme. This has allowed the Seminary to expand its reach beyond the shores of Jamaica and its two campuses, which were the main centres of learning for more than 20 years. Now, as an adjunct lecturer, I can teach from my living room by merely using my computer to access the internet.

Key Proverb: *A decision made at night may be changed in the morning.* —Samoan Proverb

40. Be Confident to Win

The words of Jamaica's first national hero, Marcus Garvey, speak to this key: "Without confidence, you are twice defeated in the race of life." When we are not confident, we tend to feel that we can't take on challenges. We encounter defeat mentally and then our actions confirm it. It is the confident who will tackle problems. It is the confident who will persevere. It is the confident who will exercise creativity and take risks. Low confidence or lack of confidence robs us of the power to fulfil our potential.

However, the good news is that confidence is a learnable skill that can be cultivated. Confidence grows in the soil of competence and clarity. It grows with experience. Confidence grows in the soil of encouragement. Confidence grows in the soil of self-awareness and having a sense of purpose and mission in life. It grows out of a proper understanding of one's identity and taking action to conquer fear. Therefore, let's *Be Confident to Win*.

Real Life Application: When Sally first started driving, she would not travel on certain routes, especially those with long winding roads. With practice, Sally gained confidence and today drives just about anywhere by herself. Her competence and experience have given her the confidence to do so.

Key Proverb: *In quietness and in confidence shall be your strength.* —Bible Proverb

41. Be Efficient and Reliable to Win

This speaks to doing your job well in good time and keeping your word. It speaks to managing your personal resources and that of others well. John Maxwell has written a book titled *Talent is Never Enough*. This book emphasizes the point that most people who succeed in life were never the most talented or skilled, but they worked harder than most and exercised certain basic skills and principles of discipline. They became efficient in what they did and became reliable. I'm sure you know some persons who are extremely talented but not dependable. If you give them a job to do, they will not complete it in time or do it well.

When you are not reliable or efficient, you will not attract success. In business, you will lose clients. In relationships, you will become untrustworthy, and people will not be able to vouch for you. On the other hand, those who are reliable and efficient will be promoted, and their good reputation will open many doors for them. People feel safe in relationships with persons who are reliable and efficient. Therefore, make it your business to develop a reputation of being reliable and efficient to win at life.

Do not just apply this key to yourself but also when working as part of a team or putting a team together. Seek reliable and efficient persons or else you will have difficulty completing your targets and sustaining your organization.

Real Life Application: Fiverr.com has become my favourite outsourcing platform, because the workers I have contracted are efficient and reliable. My publishing partners, N.D. Author Services are very efficient and reliable. They deliver quality and affordable work on time. This has caused me less stress in the publishing process, and I have confidently recommended their services to others.

Key Proverb: *Cyaan bury ah man an lef out im foot.* (Translation: You cannot bury a man and leave out his feet.) —Jamaican Proverb

42. Be Patient to Win

The phrase "strong trees don't grow overnight" reminds me to be patient when I begin to become impatient in the process of striving for success. A short-cut mindset is one of the top reasons for failure. This is the *instant generation*, but the things which are built to last often take time. This is true in building your career, developing character, learning a skill or building wealth, in as much as it is true that diamonds take years to form. We have to be patient with ourselves and others to win. A baby is not conceived and born the same day.

In the same way, learn to exercise patience with yourself. Bad habits are not unlearnt in a day. Failure to wait is one of the top reasons for debt. A lack of patience is the reason why we sacrifice long-term gain for short-term gratification. I've had to learn the hard way that that which is built slowly lasts longer, even in this instant generation. That which takes longer to gain is often more protected and treasured. There is no such thing as an overnight success. The recognition usually comes long after many years of practice behind the scene. Therefore, *Be Patient to Win*.

Real Life Application: Two years ago, I visited a couple who lived in a very beautiful house in an upscale community. This couple were both over fifty years of age. I then asked them about how they went about purchasing and acquiring their home. Their answer was interesting. They built it overtime, bit by bit over a period of 10 years. The couple did not owe any mortgage on the house. I was impressed by the story of their diligence and patience in pursuing their dream home without being indebted.

Patience does have its rewards. In this case, it is acquiring a home debt free.

Key Proverb: *The moon moves slowly but it crosses the town.* —African Proverb

43. Be Willing to Fail to Win

Many of us are perfectionists. We are waiting for the perfect weather to plant our crops or to perfect our craft before displaying it. However, I find that this can be one of the surest ways to not succeed. I believe like Les Brown, that if a thing is worth doing any at all, it is worth doing wrong until you get it right, if you do not know how to do it right. We learn more from failure than we do from success. In our failures, we gain experience and new insights that help us to refine our ideas and perfect our craft.

The baby who learnt to walk fell many times. It is in the process of trial and error that we often learn the most. Success experts like Darren Hardy, in fact, encourage people to fail often and to fail fast to speed up your chances of success. Take a chance today. You may fail, but you will learn, and this knowledge may help you to win faster.

Real Life Application: When I delivered my first speech over fifteen (15) years ago, I was not any good at it and I was not paid for it. I still remember it with some embarrassment, but that experience was part of my training. I did not give up speaking after that; today, I speak frequently to hundreds, and in many cases the reception has been phenomenal. Speaking is now part of my income stream. Had I not been willing to fail, my gift would not have been honed to the extent that I am earning from it.

Key Proverb: *To get lost is the way to learn.*
—African Proverb

44. Beat Fear to Win

It is said that in the Bible, there are 365 commands to fear not. I believe that is one for every day of the year. Fear is a crippling emotion and one of the chief reasons for failure. Whether it be fear of old age, fear of success, fear of failure, fear of loss of love, fear of poverty, fear of criticism or rejection, justified or not, these fears are obstacles to our success. They often hold us captive, keep us in unhealthy environments and keep our talents buried.

One way to beat fear is to take action. Action conquers fear. We perhaps cannot get rid of fear, but as psychologist and author Susan Jeffers encourages, we should feel the fear and do it anyway. This is one proven way to beat fear. Act on the thing you fear, and the death of fear is sure. Very often after I act, I find myself saying, *"this was not so scary after all. I should have done it much sooner."*

Real Life Application: If anyone knows about fear, I do. I was the queen of being afraid—afraid of the dark even as an adult, afraid of people, afraid of new surroundings, afraid of new experiences and so many other things. Fear crippled me so much so that when I was asked to be Valedictorian at my High School leaving exercise, I said "no." Who turns down an honour like that? Fear robs us of opportunities. However, today, I am less fearful and am a public speaker, speaking to change lives. All of this would not have been possible, if I were still held captive by fear.

Key Proverb: *Do not let what you cannot do tear from your hands what you can.* — African Proverb

45. Become an Inverse Paranoid to Win

I first heard this term from Brian Tracy, but the idea is not new. The idea here is to think that all things are working for your good no matter what happens. It is a fancy way of re-framing the Apostle Paul's advice to the Roman Christians: "That all things work together for good to them that love God and are called according to his purpose" (Romans 8:28). It's an outlook on life that breathes hope and helps you to deal with life's problems in a better frame of mind. Somehow this kind of thinking fortifies you and helps you to see the silver lining in every cloud. This kind of thinking wards off depression and is worthy of adoption. This kind of thinking does wonders for your emotional health.

Real Life Application: Five years ago, John was fired from his job, which he had held for many years. However, John's desire had always been to become a police officer. When he lost his job, his friends told him to view it as an opportunity or a gift in disguise. Although it was painful, John's release was the opportunity for him to pursue his real passion: becoming a police officer. Today, John serves in the Jamaican police force, and this might not have happened if he had not been fired.

Key Proverb: *Nothing so bad as not to be good for something.* —German Proverb

46. Beware of the "Spoilers" to Win

There are the spoilers within and the spoilers without. The term "spoiler" was used by Jim Rohn to describe the enemies of your progress. There is both good and evil in this world. There are those who will plot your downfall. This world has thieves and murderers, and you need to beware so you can take precaution and protect yourself. However, some of the most effective spoilers are not people but bad habits and attitudes that will destroy your life. For example, constantly eating junk food; lack of exercise and smoking. There are other spoilers like fear and self-doubt; worry, anxiety and other negative attitudes which will not enable you to win at life.

The internal spoilers are like the weeds which will destroy your garden, if you leave it un-attended. There is an African proverb that says "if there is no enemy within, the enemy without can do you no harm." Watch out for the spoilers within, especially the crippling story we tell ourselves about our inactions or bad decisions. Watch out for others such as self-pity, blame, resentment, laziness, bitterness and un-forgiveness will destroy us from within. We should be very wary of them.

Real Life Application: Jack's father was an alcoholic, and Jack remembers how this habit negatively impacted his family life. Jack made a pact from an early age that he would never become an alcoholic. Today Jack has a stable family and has not repeated his father's error. He was mindful of that particular spoiler.

Key Proverb: *The very thing that killed a mother rat is always there to make sure that its young ones never open their eyes.*
—African Proverb

47. Bounce it to Win

This key is an amazing key which is to be used wisely. *Bounce it to Win* can be used in several senses. It can be used to get feedback from others and to make wise decisions. As the Bible proverb says, *in the multitude of counsel there is safety*. Your ideas always seem right until they are heard and challenged. This is why it is good to hear the opinions of others but not necessarily be swayed by them. You must still make up your mind in the end but at least your decision will be informed. When you bounce ideas it helps you to refine your ideas.

In writing this book, I formed a *Design to Win Facebook Community*, where in I shared the keys and my book design ideas. The feedback from Community members helped to refine the keys and book design. Members of the community showed me things I never saw and gave me useful information that I never knew. Bouncing is a good way of testing a product before mass producing it. However, let me warn you...

If you are not prepared to follow advice, it will be difficult. If you are inflexible or fearful of criticism, it will be difficult to apply.

Real Life Application: In 2016, I was part of a team planning a major event for students who were scheduled to graduate in a few months. After months of preparation, we presented a copy of the "final" programme to the Principal for him to see that we had blundered with some things. Of course, I was a little put off on the eve of the event, and then I remembered the key: "Bounce it to Win."We did not "bounce" the final draft with the Principal. Therefore, there was no need for me to get upset. I should have known better. This is actually good. You see, it is as Les Brown says: "You cannot see yourself in the mirror when you are in the frame." In the audience of one, everything seems right. In the end, bouncing it with the Principal saved us from certain challenges which could have occurred at the event.

Key Proverbs: *The fly that has no one to advise him, follows a corpse into the grave.* — African Proverb

48. Change Yourself to Win

This is very often the position I take with difficult people or in situations which are unchangeable or in relationship with persons who refuse to change. It is a key learnt from author Jim Rohn: "For things to change, you have to change." If you cannot change the people or situation, change yourself. You change how you speak and act towards the person or the situation. It's like learning to set a better sail.

Don't quarrel about the heat of the sun; that's what the sun is made to do. Wear sunscreen lotion or bring an umbrella. Don't complain about things you cannot change. Change how you handle the situation. I find this attitude and action helps to reduce stress and, in some cases, the other individual changes. This key reduces conflict, helps us to get along better with others and reduces internal stress.

Real Life Application: Nancy was always complaining that at the end of each month, there was no money after getting paid and paying the bills. After listening to Dave Ramsey's teaching on personal finances, Nancy decided to follow his principles. Her salary did not increase, and yet for the first time in years, Nancy now has money saved in her bank account. Her job did not change, but she changed her money habits, and now she is doing better financially.

Key Proverb: *A mountain cannot turn but a road can.* —Chinese Proverb

49. Diagnose to Win

This is learning like a doctor to get to the root of your problem. If you are angry, ask yourself: "Why am I angry? What is at the root of my anger?" Many times the situation to which we are reacting is not the problem; it is just a trigger. When we get to the root of the problem, it is then we can treat it. Don't be too quick to give a solution to a problem that you have not taken time to diagnose.

Many of us are struggling with some issues that started way back in childhood, and unless we get to the root of it, we will continue to struggle. Like a doctor, when we see symptoms of a disease, we should try to find the root cause. This may mean tracking our family history and our personal history since childhood to find patterns and incidents connected to the present behaviour. When did this habit or pattern first begin? What happened when it first occurred or normally occurs? Using this key can lead to greater self-awareness and insight. You cannot treat what you cannot label, and for some persons, just having a label or gaining understanding often brings relief.

Real Life Application: For many years, no matter how much I achieved, I never felt I was good enough. I felt unloved, unwanted and insignificant, and I just could not understand it. In 2013, while I was in Namibia, Africa, I did a course via a series of seminars called *Family Foundations*. It was during that course, as I examined my family history, that I realized the root of my problem and found a sense of freedom.

This deep seated feeling of rejection and tendency towards perfectionism stemmed from my early childhood experiences of being separated from my mother and father and was due to a particular tragic event which occurred when I was five years old. These events are described in my autobiography *Heartache Queen Unshackled*. This understanding or diagnosis has helped me tremendously to treat with issues of rejection and inferiority.

Key Proverb: *When a man fails to realize where rain started beating him he cannot predict where it will stop.* —African Proverb

50. Establish Boundaries to Win

The proverb "familiarity breeds contempt" comes to mind with this key or "give someone an inch and they take a mile." This key is necessary to prevent abuse and to protect one's self or others from getting hurt. Sometimes it is only after our feelings have been hurt or we have been abused or treated with scant regard, that we set up the boundaries. Setting up boundaries includes not permitting persons to speak to you in demeaning ways; it means letting people know early on what behaviours you will tolerate and what you will not tolerate. It means setting clear lines of demarcation or establishing rules or standards and making them known to others.

Setting up boundaries can protect the vulnerable. Laws are boundaries, and police officers are enforcers. In our personal lives, we should do the same. Boundaries can be established by outlining expectations and establishing roles and responsibilities and a hierarchy of management. Establishing boundaries also plays a role in being resilient. It may not come naturally for some persons, but it is necessary. Let's do this before it is too late.

Real Life Application: Pat was tired of the disrespect she was receiving from her co-worker. One day she had a talk with that co-worker and told her she would no longer put up with her behaviour. This made things uncomfortable at work but now Pat is less distressed and her co-worker thinks twice before doing certain things.

Key Proverb: *Respect is greater from a distance.* —Latin Proverb

51. Express (share) it to Win

This key speaks to sharing your emotions instead of repressing them. Dr. David Clark in his book, *Six Steps to Emotional Freedom*, encourages the act of expressing our significant emotions whether positive or negative rather quickly for our own emotional health.

He explains that if the emotion is significant, meaning that the feeling lingers or the event continues to affect you for 24-48 hours, that it is a significant, and the emotions should be expressed. Many people repress their negative feelings, and this creates internal stress which often causes bitterness and illnesses such as heart attack, ulcers, depression, etc. Whether the emotion is positive or negative, it should be expressed in a healthy manner.

Express it to Win also speaks to being vulnerable, because healing takes place in community. In sharing one often finds relief, because after all we are social beings. Having someone to talk to and airing your feelings really does help to reduce stress. Sometimes especially for ladies, we do not need advice, just a listening ear and the problem is "solved." Is it any wonder we have so many counsellors and psychologists? This is in fact, paying to talk to someone, and by talking we are able to diagnose our condition and get the help and treatment needed.

Real Life Application: For many years, I was afraid of my mother. When I was around her even as an adult, I was very timid. It was my fiancé who pointed out that when I was around my mom that I became like a little child. Eventually, I decided to exercise courage and let my mother know how I felt about certain things, and I did so in writing. This act, somehow released me from the fear that held me captive for so many years. Today, mom and I have a really great relationship, and I can express myself freely to her, even when I disagree with her opinions.

Key Proverb: *It is better to blush than to keep the concern in your heart.* —African Proverb

52. Fail Forward to Win

This is a key named after John Maxwell's book, *Failing Forward*. The idea here is to see failure as a motivator and a platform for success. If we choose to learn from our failures, we may learn lessons that accelerate our success. The more you fail, the more you will learn what not to do and, by process of elimination, you should be closer to the right result. Failure is often a great teacher, if we use it wisely, and we don't give up when we fail. We have to see failures as further attempts in learning to get the right results. To fail forward is to let failure inform your next action instead of letting failure defeat you.

Real Life Application: Financial expert Dave Ramsey's story illustrates this point. Over 20 years ago, he and his wife filed for bankruptcy. The experience of being bankrupt led Ramsey on a journey of learning to master his personal finances. He embarked on a path that eventually re-established his family's finances, and today those lessons learnt have been used to help millions of others to come out of debt. These lessons have been mastered by his children, and thus he has changed his family tree.

Key Proverb: *Allow the breeze that brought a maize plant down to strengthen it.* — African Proverb

53. Focus and Concentrate to Win

No matter how good your camera is, if it is not focussed, the images will not be good. It is the same way in life. We often talk about multi-tasking and boast about our ability to do so, but I find multi-tasking does not increase your efficiency or speed. In fact, it often takes longer to get the task done. If we do things one at a time and concentrate, we get more done.

When you decide to specialize in an area, you are being focussed. You will learn more and will stand out more when you do this, rather than trying to learn everything. You cannot be an expert cricketer and a basket-ball player at the same time. You have to choose and concentrate on one, or you end up a 'Jack of all trades and master of none.' Those who are successful have learnt the importance of focus and the power of concentration. Apply this key to your life to experience greater productivity.

Real Life Application: I find in the mornings that, as long as I stay away from social media, reduce the use of my Smartphone and my computer, that I can complete my morning routine in time to reach work early. Whenever I stop to check emails or Facebook, my activities take longer, and I run the risk of being late. My morning routine includes making breakfast, spending time in prayer and getting a few other things done, which can all be done in 2 hours. However, when I am distracted, something is usually left undone, and I have to rush to arrive at work on time.

Key Proverb: *The hunter who is tracking an elephant does not stop to throw stones at birds.* —African Proverb

54. Forgive to Win

Despite the fact that human beings often commit egregious and horrible acts one towards another, forgiveness is still required to win. Unforgiveness hurts the victim more than it does the perpetrator. Unforgiveness is like swallowing poison and expecting the other person to die. Unforgiveness keeps you forever trapped in a cycle of hurt and pain.

Forgiveness does not mean forgetting or even letting the guilty go free. Forgiveness does not mean reconciliation. Forgiveness is a decision to let go of the debt of hurt, resentment and anger towards the perpetrator for your own sake. Holding on to anger and resentment has been proven to destroy a person's life and will impede your progress. The hurt virtually becomes like a god over you when you refuse to let it go.

We must learn to forgive ourselves and forgive others, if we are going to live effectively in life. Hurts will come, and we will also hurt others. We must be willing to forgive, if we want to be forgiven, whether it was an act of weakness or wickedness. It is important for our own progress, although it is perhaps the hardest key to apply.

Real Life Application: Molly has refused to let go of the past hurts and, whenever you meet her, she is always rehashing the pain of the past. This makes Molly a very difficult person to be with. Her posts on social media are usually negative, and this further isolates her. Molly also has few friends, and she is having problems getting along with her family members. If only Molly could forgive and let go of the past, her life, I believe, would be better.

Key Proverb: *He who forgives ends a quarrel.* —African Proverb

55. Go the Extra Mile to Win

This key is often the luck factor. It is the habit of doing more than paid for and one of success expert Napoleon Hill's seventeen (17) laws of success. I have named my company after this principle. Those who go the extra mile will get noticed. If you come in earlier and work longer, you will get noticed, and that may give you the edge over someone else when it's time for a promotion. It is like planting seeds and overtime you reap the rewards. The student who submits his work before the due date is going the extra mile. When we give a "brawta" in Jamaica, that is, giving something extra beyond what is purchased, that's going the extra mile. You tend to win the favour of others by it. When you do more than is generally accepted, it is going the extra mile, and it will bring reward eventually. Try it today.

Real Life Application: In 2013, I changed my travel agent, because my new travel agent went the extra mile. Not only did he find airfares at lower rates, but he would offer mobile service and come to my office to offer his service. Since then I have recommended many clients to him, and they too have gotten the extra mile service. Recently an individual I recommended gave me rave reviews about him. It really does pay to go the extra mile.

Key Proverb: *He who is outside his door has the hardest part of his journey behind him.* —Dutch Proverb

56. Keep it in Sight to Win

Jim Rohn once said, "Everything by longevity tends to go off track." Keeping your goal in sight will help you to stay on track. This can be done in a number of ways. The important thing is to do something that will cause you to remember your purpose, goals and priorities.

For example, as it relates to goal setting, some people create vision boards, some have cards that they review several times a day, some record their dreams and visions and play these back repeatedly, some people walk around with physical items as reminders of what is important and some daily re-write their goals. The manner you choose to keep it in sight does not matter, as long as you do so to stay on track.

Real Life Application: I would have all but gone off course many times, if it had not been for my folder of my dreams and vision, which I created in 2014. In this folder are not only written goals but pictures and images to remind me of my goals. I review it often to stay on track. I find too that when I rewrite my major goals daily, as Brian Tracy teaches, that I tend to be more focussed and effective, and I find more opportunities to fulfil my goals.

Key Proverb: *Mankind is made out of forgetfulness.* —Arabian Proverb

57. Learn to Say "No" to Win

This is another key that is hard to apply. However, If we do not develop the backbone to say "no," we may end up being unproductive, abused, overworked and feel greatly dissatisfied. There are persons who for fear of the loss of a relationship always say "yes," and then they cannot deliver their promises. This only hurts your reputation and credibility. There are those who are so addicted to approval that saying "no" is like a dirty word. In the end we only hurt ourselves by always saying "yes." We cannot excel in an area without saying "no" to other areas.

In order to win at life, our "yeses" should be few and our "nos" many. Not learning to say "no" to the trivial many will lead to failure. We cannot say "yes" to every purchase, if we want to become financially independent. Neither can we say "yes" to every charity and every event. Learning to say "no" is an important step in becoming disciplined.

We cannot do everything we want to do, when we want to, if we plan to succeed. We must learn to say "no" more often for greater focus and output. It will take courage and wisdom to apply this key, but it will be more rewarding when it is applied.

Real Life Application: My failure to say "no" has resulted in much pain over the years. There are things that I regret, because I did not have the courage to say "no." I am however learning, and even while writing this book, I had to say "no" to two speaking engagements in order to focus on completing this task. If I did not say no, this manuscript would have taken a longer time to finish.

Key Proverb: *A slave has no choice.* —African Proverb

58. List it to Win

I learnt this key from author, Brian Tracy. "When feeling listless, make a list." This is one of my most used keys. Every week I make a list of all my things to do, and then I assign myself 5-6 major things to do daily. This helps me sleep better at nights and helps me run my day instead of my day running me. When this is done, I don't wake up wondering what to do, and if I do forget, I simply go for my list.

This key helps me when I have a project to do. I list all that needs to be done and attack it in phases or steps. It works like a charm. By listing, I tend not to forget the important things that need to be done. I don't have to panic at the last minute, because I have tried beforehand to think through all the possibilities, and I write them down in list format. If I am not present, someone should be able to easily substitute for me, because I have listed what needs to be done.

Listing facilitates delegating and outsourcing. Listing keeps you on track. Listing can become a useful activity to engage in when waiting in a line. "When feeling listless, make a list." For example, while waiting, make a "to do" list. List your major life goals and dreams on paper or Smartphone. Listing will increase your personal efficiency, reduce your stress levels and will become a major productivity tool for you. How will you utilize this key?

Real Life Application: When I am at work, I constantly think about what is needed next, and then I make a *to do* list. This habit has helped us to meet our major targets and keeps us on track.

Key Proverb: *Let there be writing before you pay, and receipt before you write.* —Spanish Proverb

59. Look for the Benefit to Win

It was success expert, Napoleon Hill that said, "There is a seed of equivalent benefit in every adverse situation." One way of handling challenging negative situations is by looking for the benefit in them. You do this by asking questions such as:

- How could this work for my good?
- What lesson could I learn?
- How could this experience help me to help someone else?

Sometimes the things which happen to you are not for you but for others. Your pain could become a platform for your greatness in that the very thing you struggle with and conquer, may very well be the thing that helps you to help others. You then become what psychologist Carl Jung refers to as a "wounded healer."

Many persons in the helping professions today are there because of the suffering they experienced and their own search for healing. Now that they are healed, they seek to help others to do the same. Some say 70% of psychologists are wounded healers.

Problems force us to find solutions. Author, Myles Munroe once said that "Every business is a solution to a problem." For example, the solution to the inconvenience of walking long distances is the invention of cars and other modes of transportation. The invention of the washing machine is because of the inconvenience or problem of washing by hand, and the list goes on and on. Discomfort, discovery and invention go together. In fact, every job is based on a problem to be solved. Think about it! Perhaps we should not despise our problems so much after all.

Real Life Application: It was Dave Ramsey's problem of bankruptcy which led to the solutions which he captured in his book, *Total Money Makeover*, which became a best-seller and a tool that has helped millions. The solution to his financial problem resulted in a talk show, now aired on over 500 stations in the United States and Canada.

Key Proverb: *Hungry mek monkey blow fire.* (Translation: Hunger makes a monkey blow fire.) —Jamaican Proverb

60. Own it to Win

Admit your shortcomings, weaknesses and failures. This is the first step in getting help and healing. If you are in denial, you cannot be helped. Only by acknowledging will you take steps to fix it. Acknowledge you have a problem and need help. Acknowledge your past mistakes.

Acknowledge and face the hurt and the pain, if you want to be healed. Don't repress the pain. Don't deny your part in the matter. Confession is good for the soul. No wonder the writer of the book of James encouraged his Christian brethren to confess their faults one to another and pray for one another so that they could be healed. This key is calling us to see the situation for what it is before we can treat it.

Real Life Application: Those who are part of Alcoholics Anonymous will tell you that the first step to getting better is admitting that you are an alcoholic. Without admission, there can be no change. Admission has been a key part of their successful twelve (12) step programme for years. It also dawned on me, that even in becoming a Christian, we first have to admit that we are sinners, before we can accept God's offer of salvation.

Key Proverb: *For no man could be blessed without the acceptance of his own head.* — African Proverb.

61. Persevere to Win

This is a key I learnt from listening to the stories of people who have been successful in their businesses and also from little children. For example, Jack Canfield, author of *Chicken Soup for the Soul*, was rejected by 130 publishers before his book was accepted, and today it holds the Guinness Book record as one of the bestselling books of all times. To persevere means we keep trying until....

Every dream will be tested, and if you cannot persevere you cannot win. Children, for example, will nag you until they get what they want. Adults, on the other hand, when rejected once or twice tend to give up because of pride. Nevertheless, if the dream matters, you will persevere despite the odds. You will persevere when your goals are backed by strong compelling reasons. If the prize is compelling enough, we will pay the price to get it. If you intend to persevere, make your reason (s) compelling. Be like a child learning to walk, keep trying though you fall many times, because one day you will walk.

Real Life Application: My mother epitomizes this key. When she was preparing to matriculate to Nursing school, she had a problem with Mathematics and English. Mom failed Math four times before she finally passed her Caribbean Council Examination. English was harder, she finally passed it after about seven attempts. She refused to give up, and today she is reaping the rewards.

Key Proverb: *Dripping water eventually wears away stone.* —Chinese Proverb

62. Remove the Personal Effects to Win

Many of us often see criticism or unfavourable responses as a personal attack. If we are going to win at life, it is of utmost importance that we learn not to take things too personally. Sometimes the person who is behaving irritably or treating you badly is not doing so because of you. Often times, they are having personal problems. Therefore, we need to train ourselves to find ways and means to reduce the pain that comes with criticism or negative responses.

We should learn to appropriate responsibility, that is, know when to take the blame and when not to. We should learn to laugh at ourselves when we make silly mistakes and not allow our feelings to be hurt so easily. Don't take everything people say too seriously.

Know that sometimes the reaction or situation may have nothing to do with your competence or character; it's just the situation and the way things are. This kind of thinking helps us to react more objectively and deal more effectively in adverse situations.

Real Life Application: Romaine was obviously not in a good mood. He refused to carry out my instructions in class, and I was getting angrier by the minute. Then I remembered the key *Remove the Personal Effects to Win.* I remembered the importance of not taking his behaviour as a personal indictment of my abilities. I said to myself:

> *After all, I am teaching adult students, and thus if he refuses to listen, that is his problem. It is more a reflection of his character and, in the end, it will only hurt him. Adults are responsible for their behaviour.*

With this kind of thinking, I resumed my lesson. *It's nothing personal. I know I am a good teacher, and one uncooperative adult student does not change that.*

Key Proverb: *There can be no offense where none is taken.* —Japanese Proverb

63. Run Your Own Race to Win

This speaks to eliminating the destructive habit of comparing ourselves to others or trying to be like others instead of ourselves. We often compare our gifts and abilities instead of celebrating our uniqueness and maximizing our gifts the best way we know how. You don't stand out by trying to be like everyone else. You get noticed by what sets you apart from the crowd.

While you should emulate the qualities and the principles of the successful, you should still be yourself and make your own mark. Failure to do so is a reflection of low self-esteem and an inferiority complex, which leads to always thinking you are not as good as John or Mary and therefore you should not attempt that thing. Failure to run your own race may cause you live beyond your means, because you are trying to live like the Joneses. You may end up in a cycle of people pleasing and always feeling like a misfit.

Comparison defeats contentment and leads to ingratitude. I've had to remind myself that I am not like everyone else. My race is different, and I will run my course. In track and field, if you cross someone else's lane, you will be disqualified. If you stop focussing on the finish line and start watching others instead of running your own race, you are most likely to lose. Celebrate who you are and go at your own pace. You are not like everyone else. Be the best version of you and run your own race.

Real Life Application: I must admit this is a key I struggle with very often. Sometimes I look at my age and my achievements when compared to others and I feel terrible. I have to fight the green-eyed monster in me, and that feeling of being discontent when I see others doing better, especially financially and vocationally. This key to run my own race is what keeps me steady. Each of us has a different path, and I will run my own race.

Key Proverb: *To compare is not to prove.* — French Proverb

64. Stay Calm to Win

Over the years, I have had anxiety attacks, panic attacks and a bad temper. I have learnt the hard way that being calm is definitely more effective and more respected. So when I find myself getting 'hot under the collar,' I ask myself: why am I getting angry? Why does it matter? What is the trigger? What's the root?

Anger is always a signal to something else. Getting to the root of it helps. Sometimes the root is rejection, fear, shame or embarrassment, but once you find the root you can treat with it. I've noticed in arguments that the one who stays calm is treated with more respect. In times of distress and crisis, staying calm is critical. It is vital for problem solving and is an admirable trait of a good leader.

When we are emotional, we cannot think straight. We don't make logical decisions or act right. Sometimes we say words we regret and cannot take back. Sometimes we act violently and, after the act, we have deep regrets. Therefore I implore you to *Stay Calm to Win!*

Real Life Application: My colleague came through the door sighing and heaving at the feedback from her Boss. I too became a little 'hot under the collar' and began complaining angrily. Apparently, my colleague had come back to her senses, because she told me to calm down. In that instant, my mind shifted to the keys: *Stay Calm to Win* and *Look for the Benefit in Every Situation.* I really should have known better. True to form, the Boss's response had some validity and with some measure of calmness returning to my mind, I was able to act on the recommendation and the problem was solved.

Key Proverb: *The one who knows much says little; an understanding person remains calm.* —Bible Proverb

65. Think Abundance to Win

I learnt this key from author and virtual mentor, Michael Hyatt on one of his podcasts. The podcast is called, "This is your Life." He learnt it from his wife to combat a scarcity mindset which often leads to fear and worry. When he gets into scarcity mode, she normally says: "There's more where that came from."

Trust me, this simple phrase has helped to calm me many times since I learnt it. Whenever I think that I am going to lose something, I repeat the phrase and the worry ceases. If I think I am not going to get another contract, no more favors or feel that someone has stolen something from me, I repeat the phrase and I feel better.

I strongly recommend becoming an abundant thinker. This kind of mindset is one that not only seeks to produce enough to take care of ourselves and our families, but it requires thinking and producing more than enough to take care of others. It's that cup running over mentality. It is also a mindset that deters greed, because you will say to yourself: there is enough for all of us. Try it today and see how it works for you.

Real Life Application: Donna lost a vital member of her network and was somewhat disappointed. I told her to think abundantly: "There's more where that came from. I'm sure that member can be replaced." Sure enough, that very week Donna found a replacement and was happy with the new member of the group.

Key Proverb: *Where a river flows, there is abundance.* —Nilotic Proverb

66. Think "this too will pass" to Win

No problem lasts forever. Whenever you are facing an unbearable situation, encourage yourself with the thought that "this too will pass." It's raining now, but the sun will shine again. This kind of thinking has helped to calm my fears and make the present situation bearable. One day it will be no more. This kind of thinking gives hope for the future, which is an essential ingredient for success.

Real Life Application: My heart was broken. My hopes for marriage had been dashed to pieces, and my tears were flowing like a river. It was hard to believe that I would ever smile again but I did. I was mindful of the fact that "this too will pass." Others have triumphed over despair and so can I. Read more in my autobiography, *Heartache Queen Unshackled*.

Key Proverb: *However long the night, the dawn will break.* —African Proverb

67. Track it to Win

This is about keeping scores in any area of your life that you think needs improvement. It is also a good way to measure your progress. Tracking helps you get the facts. For example, if you are having financial problems, why not track your expenses for a month by recording every penny you spend for 31 days? At the end of the 31 days, categorize the expenses and see how much you are spending in each area. Then look to see where you can trim your expenses or where you are wasting money, then you can make adjustments.

The same thing works with your time, habits, history, experiences, grades or any area that requires evaluation. Do an analysis over a set time period to gather the facts, so you can have accurate data to evaluate and make adjustments. Tracking could also be a simple mental exercise to find the answer to a problem or account for your progress. This is a fantastic strategy to improve your life.

Real Life Application: In 2015, I tracked my expenses for 31 days and was shocked by the results. I did this in an effort to improve my personal finances. According to the results, I was spending approximately 25% of my income on a particular mode of transportation which was quite costly, and I did not have to! The tracking on paper helped me to see clearly the evidence of a 13 year old habit that was robbing me of financial health. At that moment, I made some crucial decisions which reduced my travel expenses to about 5% of my income.

Key Proverb: *Know well the condition of your flocks, and give attention to your herds.* —Bible Proverb

68. See the Whole Picture to Win

When we are discouraged or in shock, we often use one situation to make a false generalizations. I came up with a phrase that has often helped me to regain perspective: *"Don't let the moment drown out the whole."* The more common phrase is to *"separate the trees from the forest."*

Don't use one failed scenario to label everything as a failure. Is the thing you are worried about really important in the larger scheme of things? Is what you are looking at true in every instance? Is your evaluation true in all cases? When we apply this key, it will prevent us from making bad judgements and also lift us out of despair and worry.

Furthermore, when we see how what we are doing contributes to the whole, we make wiser decisions. When we see the whole picture, we will live intentionally. For example, you may be feeling small, because you are merely an office attendant, but if you see that task in the larger scheme of doing something to contribute to the success of the company, you may feel better about your role and change your work attitude for the better. When you can connect what you are doing to the bigger picture it generally gives you a boost. On the converse side, when you can't see how your little part impacts on the whole, it can be discouraging. *See the Whole Picture to Win today!*

Real Life Application: It was Lisa's first term in graduate school, and it was a stressful period. On her first test, she got a "C" and was devastated, having been a straight "A" student in her undergraduate programme. Lisa was encouraged by looking at the whole picture, because even though she did not get an "A" on that quiz, she could still pass the course with a good grade. In the end, Lisa got a "B+" for the course. Thus that moment did not drown out the whole.

Key Proverb: *Don't make mountains out of mole hills.* —English Proverb

IDENTITY AND INVESTMENTS

"He that is wise will hear, and will increase learning; and the intelligent will gain wise counsels"
—African Proverb

These eighteen (18) keys will help to shape your identity and showcase the investments you need to make along your life journey in order to win at life.

69. Win with Self- Acceptance

This key speaks to being comfortable in one's skin; that is, being at peace with who you are. It does not mean you do not strive for change, but it means you know who you are: your strengths, weaknesses, likes and dislikes, your mistakes and successes, and you embrace these qualities as things that make you unique. Self-acceptance is an important factor in building self-esteem and confidence, without which it is difficult to progress. Those who refuse to accept themselves are often unhappy, always comparing themselves to others and trying to be like someone else. The Irish playwright Oscar Wilde said: "Be who you are because everyone else is taken." If you don't accept who you are, why should others do so?

Real Life Application: My friend Cindy has come to terms with her disability. As a teen-ager she lost the ability to walk. However, this has not prevented her from living a meaningful life. Cindy learnt a skill instead of becoming a beggar. She has also worked hard on her physical condition with exercise and proper dieting. Today, Cindy is a fairly independent woman, earning an income, paying her own bills and taking care of her needs. She has accepted herself and is a blessing to many.

Key Proverb: *No matter how long a log stays in water, it does not become a crocodile.* — African Proverb

70. Win with Self-Care

When travelling on the airlines, one of the safety instructions given is this: "If there is an accident, put on your mask first before help-ing others." If you cannot breathe you cannot help others.

Self-care is not being selfish. It is ensuring that you take care of yourself, so you can be of good use to others. Self-care includes learn-ing to balance a good work-rest ratio, eating well and exercising. Self–care includes feed-ing your mind with the positive and not staying in toxic relationships. Self–care includes making sure you take time out to enjoy life. Remember the proverb, "All work and no play makes Jack a dull boy."

Self-care means you don't just spend all of your money on bills. It does mean at times sacrificing to pamper yourself, so that you can function better. It means taking a vacation at regular intervals. This is one key that I have had a difficulty mastering. I suspect those who work in the helping professions also find it hard to practise. Very often we tend to neglect ourselves and those who love us need to remind us to look after ourselves. It happens in many instances to parents, especially mothers who work outside the home and in the home. However, it must be intentionally done. When we neglect to take care of ourselves, we are heading for emotional, mental and physical breakdown which in some cases may be fatal.

Real Life Application: I have learnt the value of self-care the hard way. Whenever I am overworked or not rested, I begin to suffer from pains in my neck, shoulders and back. At times I even get muscle spasms. My stomach also punishes me similarly when I am not eating properly.

About two years ago (2014), I started taking one day off each week to unplug, and it has done me wonders. After that day, I usually think clearer and feel refreshed.

Key Proverb: *When crab walk too much,'im lose 'im claw.* (Translation: A crab which walks too much loses its claw.) —Jamaican Proverb

71. Win with Self-Worth

It was business philosopher and author, Jim Rohn, who really captured the importance of this key for me in one of his presentations: "The understanding of self-worth is the beginning of progress." Learning this key has been liberating for me. For a long time, I was blind to my worth, thinking less of myself because of my race, social class, lack of material possessions and the perceptions of others. I realize that when we are blind to our own worth, we become victims of abuse in some form, and we end up settling for less than we deserve. When we understand our own value, we have confidence, which enhances our relationships with others and attracts more of the right kinds of people into our lives.

Since as a man thinks, so is he; if he thinks he is worth very little, his confidence will be low, and his relationships will not have much meaning. You can never maximize your potential if you believe you are of little value. Things that are of little value are treated with scant regard. If you see yourself as lacking in value, that is how you will treat yourself and others will do the same.

Every human being has dignity and worth, and my Christian world-view tells me I was made in the image of my awesome Creator, an omniscient and omnipotent being. It, therefore, means I have value and worth. That same world-view tells me I was born to rule, and people of little value are not given great responsibility. My value is even seen in my physiology.

If any of my internal organs are damaged, the cost of fixing the same is enormous. Look at the cost of doing heart surgery! Doctors have to spend years of study before they qualify to operate on the human body. Therefore, irrespective of possession or position, we are all very important as persons. When we believe this and know this deep inside, it revolutionizes our walk.

This is why my interviewer could say, "You seem to be a very confident person." This is so because after many years, I finally started to understand how valuable I am despite my historical, racial and social standing. I am valuable despite the challenges I have faced in life and even my mistakes. The more you see yourself as a valuable person, the more optimistic and positive you will be. This understanding of my worth has made my life more effective and is enabling me to win at life. If you understand your self-worth, you too can win at life.

Real Life Application: This story is told in my autobiography *Heartache Queen Unshackled*. In 2013, en route from Namibia, Africa, I was given the opportunity to travel first class, even though I had not paid for it. At that time, it was one of the most uncomfortable experiences of my life. I did not make full use of the services or enjoy the experience, because I felt I was not worthy. I started comparing myself to the other passengers in first class and missed out on a great experience. This is an experience others would have relished but I was uncomfortable because of my self-perception of my value. I did not see myself as "first class."

Key Proverb: *A beautiful thing is never perfect.* —African Proverb

72. Be Secure in Your Identity to Win

This key is akin to being self-aware, having self-worth and accepting oneself. In fact, you cannot become secure in your identity unless you are self-aware. If you don't have self-worth, you cannot be secure in your identity. The person who is secure in his/her identity is not a people pleaser and can stand up for what s/he believes in. When we are insecure in our identity, we are tossed to and fro by the whims and fancies of others. We become fearful and will be manipulated. We become like a tree without roots. Knowing who we are and understanding our purpose will make us confident, set us on the path to progress and play a role in our having a secure identity.

When you are secure in your identity, others cannot dictate who you are, and what you should or should not be doing. You will not be easily shaken by the criticism or opinions of others. You will not attack yourself when things go wrong. You will be able to walk and talk with authority. You will not necessarily feel like a misfit in certain settings. You will not necessarily feel the need to prove anything to anyone. You will find it easier to say "no."

You will be a firmly-rooted tree that can withstand the storms of life.

If you are insecure in your identity, it is time to do a self-awareness test to learn your strengths and weaknesses. It is time to consider your self-worth and begin affirming yourself by dwelling on what is good about you. In addition, find models of excellence from similar backgrounds as yours and use them to motivate yourself. Affirm your worth continually and refuse to associate with those who seek to put you down. Watch the story you tell yourself about you, because ultimately it's what you believe about yourself that makes the real difference.

Real Life Application: Nick Vuijic is an example of someone who is secure in his identity. The best-selling author and motivational speaker, has proved that it's not your physical attributes that establish your importance; it is who you are on the inside.

Nick was born without arms and legs, and yet today he is a confident individual with a wife and two children. He has embraced the things he cannot do and has made the most of what he can do. He knows he is not his limbs. This is something he had to learn over time, because as a child he was suicidal until he saw purpose in his condition. Today he is living a full life despite his disability and giving hope to many.

Key Proverb: *It is not what you are called, but what you answer to.* —African Proverb

73. Be Self-Aware to Win

Self-awareness is wrapped up in the old adage, "Know thyself." This key became more meaningful to me when I began teaching Career Guidance. One of the steps in planning your career is to do a self-assessment. When we do this, we are getting to know ourselves, our strengths and weaknesses, our personality type and tendencies. This helps in determining which career choice matches your skills and abilities and strengths.

It is difficult to choose what's best for you when you don't know yourself. It was Socrates who said, "The unexamined life is not worth living," therefore we need to examine ourselves as a pathway to designing a life worth living. The more self-aware you are the better choices you can make for yourself and others, and it should make your relationships better. Self-awareness also aids in better communication. It increases self–esteem and helps us to become more secure in our identities and increases our confidence. If you don't know who you are, you become a target for manipulation and abuse through a false perception of your own identity. S/he who is self-aware is empowered. Take a self-awareness test today. The Kiersey Temperament Sorter test is an excellent start in your journey to becoming self-aware.

Real Life Application: My students did the Kiersey temperament test, and the results were rather interesting. I could see the looks of approval, glee, surprise and understanding on their faces. Some were pleased with the results; it confirmed for many their career choices and explained certain behaviour patterns and how best to deal with their classmates. I personally found it validating and eye-opening. I realized some tendencies I have are now understandable and therefore nothing to worry about. My score interpretation validated my career choices over the years and highlighted the weaknesses that I should work on.

Key Proverb: *Monkey mus' know whe im gwine put 'im tail, before 'im order trousiz.* (Translation: A monkey must know where it's going to put its tail before it orders its trousers.) —Jamaican Proverb

74. Commit to Win

One of the causes of failure is having weak commitment. Very often when persons want to show commitment, they will make a pledge, which is a means of strengthening our word and showing seriousness. Being committed speaks to having a strong sense of focus, devotion and intention. When we are committed to something, it means we make it a priority and pledge to to stick to it despite the odds.

Every goal and every dream will be tested. Challenges are a test of our commitment. When we give up in the face of a challenge, it is a sign of weak commitment; if we have weak commitment, we will not win. Be careful to commit to the right things to thereby ensure your success in life. Success is not an overnight thing and therefore commitment will be needed to win.

Real Life Application: In 2016, Jamaica's ambassador, Dr. Shelly-Ann Fraser-Pryce, demonstrated what is meant by commitment at the Brazil Olympics. Fraser-Pryce had injured her toe, and yet she did not bow out of the 100m race. She ran through the pain with all her might and was rewarded with a bronze medal.

Key Proverb: *The creditor gets a pledge from the good payer.* —Silician Proverb

75. Develop Others to Win

This key has within it the law of reciprocity. In helping others, you are helped. The late Zig Ziglar, best-selling author and motivational speaker, said: "If you help enough people to get what they want, you will eventually get what you want." This can seem like helping people is selfish, but there is some measure of nobility in Ziglar's advice, because we are indeed here to help and serve one another.

When we help another grow, we do feel better about ourselves. Are not parents proud when they see how well their child has developed because of the role they played in that process? Is it not the teacher's greatest joy when his/her students do well and even surpass him/her? The sports coach who has prepared the team or individual for competition is happy when that individual or team wins, and yes it does come with monetary reward in many cases. Schools are built around this principle of developing others.

Furthermore, when you develop leaders especially, your influence and impact are multiplied and your legacy lives on. Developing others is one of the highest forms of service that makes life meaningful and gives you a feeling of significance.

Real Life Application: Leadership guru, John Maxwell has trained over 5 million leaders around the world. This has led to many lives around the world being transformed and also international acclaim and other rewards. One man's concern about adding value to others and investing in others has resulted in multiplied impact across continents.

Key Proverb: *The river swells with the contribution of the small streams.* —Bateke Proverb

76. Develop Yourself to Win

John Maxwell has often said, "You teach what you know but you reproduce who you are... you attract people who are like you." You cannot teach what you do not know. Developing yourself is about personal growth. It is intentionally investing in yourself to increase your value, capacity and usefulness.

As adults we no longer grow physically, but if we are to be effective, we still need to grow mentally, spiritually, emotionally, financially and relationally. The extent to which we grow in these areas will affect the quality of our lives. The more we grow in these areas, the greater our levels of influence and effectiveness.

This is the power of personal growth. When we continually invest in ourselves we will lead the field. Those who neglect their personal growth are hindering their own progress.

Real Life Application: My mother became pregnant as a teenager, but she believed in the power of personal growth to improve the quality of her life. At the age of 37, she began pursuing passes for subjects in the Caribbean Examination Council examinations. After many attempts she passed five subjects. At the age of 43, she enrolled in a nursing programme and at the age 46 graduated with a Bachelor of Science in Nursing. She later went on to specialize in Nephrology (treating patients with end stage renal failure), and today at age 53, she is once again studying to become a midwife.

She not only continues to grow academically but has grown relationally, financially, spiritually and socially. Today she is a model in her community serving them through her church's community health fairs and offering help to senior citizens. Her investment in personal growth has helped her to reap visible rewards financially, socially, academically and even spiritually.

Key Proverb: *Wealth, if you use it, comes to an end; learning, if you use it, increases.* — African Proverb

77. Give to Win

Generosity is the act of being kind and compassionate to others and having an open hand. Inasmuch as we excel in academics, in our life vocation, business and in other areas, it is important that we excel in the grace of giving in word and deed. In fact, generosity is an act of love. It is not only the diligent who prosper but also the generous.

There are studies which show that being generous reduces stress, promotes health and gives us confidence and a sense of purpose in a meaningful life. There are many have nots in this world. In fact, it is said that half of the world lives on less than US$2 per day. In a world full of selfishness, poverty, greed and all kinds of ills, generosity is needed.

I personally have benefitted tremendously from the generosity of others. It is the generosity of others that has enabled me to travel around the world, to complete my tertiary education and to serve four years as a fulltime missionary; and to whom much is given, much is required. I, therefore, have made generosity one of the core values that I practise. Therefore, I urge you to be mindful of this key.

Real Life Application: Carey anonymously paid a portion of her friend's school fee while that friend was pursuing her Bachelor's degree. Years later when Carey served as a full-time missionary, that friend became one of Carey's biggest financial supporters for several years. The financial support given by Carey's friend far out-weighed the amount Carey had paid anonymously on her friend's school fee.

Key Proverb: *What you give you get, ten times over.* —African Proverb

78. Learn More to Win

This is the whole process of engaging in self-education, because as Jim Rohn says: "Formal education will make you a living; *self-education* will make you a *fortune.*" In this information age, if you want to lead the field, remain current and relevant or improve your value and your lot in life; engaging in ongoing, life-long learning is a must. Whether this is a formal or informal process, it must be intentional. You need to be a continuous student of your industry or your field and of life. This is why successful people read daily and listen to audio programmes.

Another way of learning more to win is by attending seminars, conferences and workshops. You can use You-Tube, read magazines and books, and it need not take extra time. The act of learning can be done while travelling or while working at home and listening to an audio book or any instructional or inspiration audio material. You can read at meal times or before going to bed. For the more adventurous ones among us you can go on field trips, interview people and you can experiment to learn more. You could also become an apprentice to someone or find a mentor. In fact, the latter will accelerate your progress much faster.

As said before, the key is to intentionally engage in learning more, whether in your industry or for personal growth. Learn more about people, technology, finances, building relationships and generally how things work. This is a key to being more effective in life.

Real Life Application: My friend, Rev. Carla Dunbar, in her book *Changed: The Journey* shows how learning more really enables us to win. Having become a teenage mother at the age of 14, and having not completed high school, life looked bleak for her. However, in her thirties she returned to school, enrolled in the Jamaica Theological Seminary and completed her Bachelor's degree in Theology and Counselling.

During that time of study, she was fascinated by the taboo subject of sexual happiness and expression in marriage among Christians. Thus, she decided to do her research in that area. News of her research reached noted veteran journalist Ian Boyne, and he interviewed her. This interview catapulted her onto a public platform and national renown.

Rev. Dunbar's decision to learn more about a specific area has made her an expert, resulted in national acclaim and opened many doors for her. This is just one example of the power of learning more to win.

Key Proverb: *He who learns, teaches.* — African Proverb

79. Manage Your Emotions to Win

Almost everyday, life throws some kind of emotional bomb our way. We can't control events, but there is one thing we can control: our response. Our thinking affects our emotions, and if we control our thinking and how we interpret the disappointing situations around us, then we can control and manage our emotions.

Managing our emotions is often a matter of perspective. How we interpret or view the matter will affect how we feel because our emotions are neutral. Now, I'm not saying that because we have this key, that we will never have a meltdown, or will never show negative emotions. I am merely saying that we can learn to manage our emotions. Here are some recommendations from my personal experience for managing your emotions:

- check your thoughts
- eat right
- exercise
- feeding yourself with the truth
- give up blame
- find the benefit in the situation
- don't allow the moment to drown out the whole
- sleep if you can when feeling distressed

Your feelings should not control you. You can control them. Therefore I urge you to *Manage Your Emotions to Win.*

Real Life Application: I used to think I could not manage my emotions well. If something disappointing took place, I would refuse to go anywhere and spend several days crying or many days in a sullen state. One day, I had a fight with my fiancé about 15 minutes before a scheduled class, and I knew I could not cancel the class. I had to get it together and, to my surprise, I taught the class as if nothing had happened. Only fifteen minutes prior, I had been in great emotional distress. I learnt that day that I have more control over my emotions than I thought, and that failure to manage my emotions had been sabotaging me in the past.

Key Proverb: *A fool expresses all his emotions, but a wise person controls them.* — Bible Proverb

80. Manage your Mind to Win

Whenever I think of the mind, author Joyce Meyer's book *Battlefield of the Mind* readily comes to mind. The battle to win at life is really mind-centred. Our mind is the control centre of the body, and as author, Earl Nightingale reminds us, "we become what we think about." It is therefore important that we manage this faculty well by paying careful attention to what we think about and how we nourish our minds.

Whenever we are depressed or feeling discouraged, we should check our thoughts and what's going on in our minds. The greatest enemy is not the one outside; it is inside. It is the mismanagement of our minds.

Negative thinking results in negative behaviour and the converse is true. Mental health is just as important as physical health, or perhaps even more important. Soundness of mind is essential to win at life. Soundness of mind is not accidental, it is intentional. If we are to manage our minds effectively, we have to pay attention to our environment and make special effort to nourish our minds with things that are inspirational, wholesome and instructional.

Real Life Application: The first time I went for my driver's license, I was very nervous, thinking that I would not do well. The second time, I was in a completely different frame of mind.

I armed myself by reading *The Winning Attitude* by John Maxwell. Then I went to the examination depot with confidence in knowing that I would pass the road test. I had no doubts the second time around and, of course, I passed my road test and got my driver's license. As you can see, the two different frames of mind produced two different results.

Key Proverb: For as a man thinks in his heart so is he. —Bible Proverb

81. Master it to Win

Jamaicans are famous for athletics, especially track and field, and therefore I will use this analogy to explain this key. Have you ever noticed that prior to an athlete's winning a gold medal at the Olympics that very often s/he has difficulty getting sponsorships? But once that athlete becomes outstanding, everyone wants to come onboard! When you master your content, craft, gift or job, it will not only infuse you with a feeling of confidence; it will get you noticed and bring rewards.

Author Malcolm Gladwell says that it takes 10,000 hours of practice to master your craft. Success expert Brian Tracy notes that it takes 5-7 years of investing in your field to develop mastery of your craft, which is just about the same timeline. When you have mastered your craft, opportunities will abound. This is why author Jim Rohn said, "success is what you attract by the person you become."

If you intend to be effective in life it is wise to specialize in an area and become a master at it. Recognition comes with mastery; therefore *Master it to Win* today.

Real Life Application: John Maxwell is known worldwide for his expertise in leadership. In one of his seminars, he said, "If anyone heard me speak 30 years ago, no one would want me to speak. I was no good." In fact, Maxwell also explained that when he started out he was not a good leader, but he studied leadership, practised speaking and developed mastery in that area. The result is that in 2014, Inc. Magazine voted John Maxwell as the #1 leadership and management expert in the world! When you master it, whatever your "it" is, success naturally follows.

Key Proverb: *A man's gift makes room for him and brings him before great men.* — Bible Proverb

82. Practise to Win:

This is similar to *Master it to Win*, but its practice is not necessarily for the development of mastery. The idea here is that all skills are learnable, and if someone is better than you at something, it may just be that they have had more practice. Practising is a means of learning to get it right.

When you practise, it is a way to preserve or improve your skills, hence the phrase, "use it or lose it." Practice is a good way to decrease fear and increase your confidence. When I am doing something for the first time, very often I am nervous; I find after doing it repeatedly that I am no longer nervous. Therefore, I want to encourage you to do to *Practise to Win*.

Real Life Application: I was given 20 minutes to speak at a particular event and I did not want to mess up, so I practised the presentation several times, recording myself on my phone repeatedly in order to stay within the time limit. During these practice sessions, I was able to refine my content. When I presented at the event, I completed my presentation on time.

Key Proverb: *By trying often, the monkey learns to jump from the tree.* —African Proverb

83. Read to Win

According to motivational speaker Charlie Tremendous Jones, "You will be the same person in five years as you are today except for the people you meet and the books you *read*." The average person reads fewer than two books a year. It is often said that readers are leaders, and I believe this is true. One of the habits of ultra successful persons is daily reading. The kind of reading I am referring to in this key is intentional reading for education, information and entertainment.

Some of the benefits of reading include: boosting intelligence; increases in empathy, intelligence and brain power; relaxation; slowing the affects of Alzheimer's disease; and helping you to lead in your field. In this day of e-books and online communication, please note that reading the old fashioned way (a printed book) is more beneficial than reading online, at least according to author Andrew Dillon's research cited in an Ergonomics[6] journal, and this finding in research is increasing. Nevertheless, whether you read printed books or e-books, for information, education or entertainment, make reading a lifelong habit to win at life.

Real Life Application: In 1997, I read a book titled *Victory over the Darkness* by Neil T. Anderson, which changed my life. As a teenager I was struggling with identity issues and suicidal ideation. While reading this book, I experienced transformation as my mind was renewed. It was a watershed moment in my life. Over the years, I have read other books that have taught me many

---

[6] A. Dillon. May 2007. Ergonomics Journal. Reading from paper versus screens: a critical review of the empirical literature

different things and have enabled me to live with greater effectiveness.

Key Proverb: *Reading makes a full man, meditation a profound man, discourse a clear man.* —American Proverb

84. Review, Reflect and Evaluate to Win

This key is vital for personal accountability and growth. It also works for organizations and businesses and can be applied to every area of your life. It is similar to tracking but different in that, it is not necessarily for problem solving but for self-monitoring and evaluation or just the need to know the state of your affairs. These are some questions to bear in mind as you review, reflect and evaluate:

- What have I done well?
- What needs to be improved?
- What should be retained or changed?
- Am I meeting my targets?
- How should I move forward?

This key is also useful when testing a product, process or system. It should be done regularly as you assess your life goals, plans and even relationships. It should be done for your health and other areas of your life. Some persons reflect, review and evaluate monthly; some do so half yearly or once per year. The frequency is up to you, but I believe it's best done more than once per year. After you review, reflect and evaluate, document your findings and make plans for the future. I hope you will use this key to accelerate your progress.

Real Life Application: In 2009, I had an epiphany in which I saw my years flash before my eyes. That was the catalyst for my engagement in full-time missionary work, as I had an opportunity to review and reflect on my life. I wanted to do something to make my life count.

The result of that review, reflection and evaluation is that I enabled at least 20 others to make life changing decisions to serve beyond their homeland. Three of those persons are now married and living overseas. Lives were changed because of my period of reflection and review.

Key Proverb: *Those who rush things too much, without reflection, can be surpassed by those who take their time.* —African Proverb

85. Serve to Win

Astrophysicist Neil deGrasee Tyson is famous for this particular quotation: "We're not who we say we are, we're not who we want to be—we are the sum of the influence and impact that we have, in our lives, on others." Serving is about impacting others or doing things to benefit others. When I speak of *Serving to Win* I am not necessarily speaking of voluntary service or acts of charity and kindness; I am speaking of meeting needs or providing solutions to meet needs.

Every job is an act of service; every invention is an act of service; every business is an act of service, and the more people you serve, the more you will be rewarded. It is also true that the greater the quality of your service, the more you will win financially and influentially. Our rewards in life, says success expert, Napoleon Hill, "...are measured by the quality of our service and the quantity of our service."

This is the reason why athletes, for example, are paid more, even though the quality of their service in terms of functionality is often debated. They fill stadiums to meet the entertainment needs of millions, and therefore their rewards are greater financially. I hope you can see why serving is a key to winning at life from these examples.

Real Life Application: Mark Zuckerburg has shown us the benefits of serving many by the creation of his social media platform, Facebook, which has over one billion users. Now we can connect easily with friends and family all over the world, do business, share ideas and a whole host of other things. By helping us, he has also helped himself. Zuckerburg now has a net worth of over 56 billion dollars.

Key Proverb: *Han'go, paki come.* (Translation: Hand goes, Hand comes.) —Jamaican Proverb

86. Study to Win

Financial expert Dave Ramsey says often, "If you want to be skinny, study skinny people; if you want to be rich, study rich people." The importance of studying to win cannot be overstated. When I speak of studying, I am not merely referring to academic studies, which is a great way of mastering an area and winning at life. I am speaking generally about getting more information and making an effort to understand things better in order to be more effective.

Schooling is an expensive formal way of learning in particular areas of interest or need. What if you did this intentionally without formal education or even the expense? The benefits would be tremendous! In past times, studying meant going to a library, but with modern technology, all we have to do is to turn to Google and You-tube. The internet has made studying so much easier and therefore makes winning easier for those who will intentionally use it to be more effective in life.

If there is something you don't understand, it is time to study to win. If you want to get the best deal, win a competition, understand your opponent, understand yourself, understand a process and many other things, the answer is: *study*. Therefore I urge you to *Study to Win* today!

Real Life Application: My brother is an automotive electrician. He did not learn this skill formally in automotive school but as an apprentice to another skilled automotive technician. He studied the operations of his teacher, and today he is benefitting professionally and financially, because he was an understudy to someone who knew the trade.

Key Proverb: *Wisdom is like fire. People take it from others.* —African Proverb

RELATIONSHIPS & RESOURCES

*Wealth from get-rich-quick schemes quickly
disappears; wealth from hard work grows
over time.*
—Bible Proverb

These final fourteen (14) keys will aid us in developing the right kinds of relationships, as well as accessing and managing the resources we need to win at life. These two areas have posed the greatest challenge to me throughout my life.

87. Win with Healthy Relationships

We are relational beings, but not all relationships are good for us. We will become like the people with whom we most associate. Birds of a feather flock together. When you have healthy relationships, you can thrive.

You should assess all your relationships and ask yourself:

- Who am I becoming as a result of this relationship?
- Is it worth keeping? Am I becoming better?
- Is it helping me to achieve my goals?
- Is nourishing or draining?

It is said that 80% of our happiness depends on relationships, and so I would encourage you to preserve good relationships and not to pursue success at the expense of those relationships. However, if you realize you are in relationships with persons who are not good for you, you need an exit strategy.

Of course, if it is family, you cannot get rid of the relationship, but you can spend less time with them. If the relationship can be mended through intervention, try intervention, but if it cannot be mended, it's best to part company. Toxic relationships will ruin your life.

It was a video by Les Brown, "It's Possible" that helped me to utilize this key well. Don't let the fear of being alone cause you to stay in an unhealthy relationship. In healthy relationships, your voice is heard and your opinions are respected, you are allowed to be the best version of you, and you feel emotionally safe. You can express yourself without fear, and there is mutual care and sharing. It's time to assess your relationships and make a decision to only stay in the healthy ones.

Real Life Application: In 2010, upon hearing a teaching by Les Brown about how toxic relationships can ruin your life, I made a decision to walk away from an intimate relationship. It was hard, but I realized that relationship was not enhancing my life. I also made a decision to stay away from those who would impact me negatively.

I made a list of friends that I could count on and those I admired and decided to strengthen those relationships. This decision has enabled me to become a more confident person, and I have grown tremendously as a result. My friendships are mutually rewarding. My friends support me and I support them.

Key Proverb: *He who sows courtesy reaps friendship, and he who plants kindness gathers love.* —Spanish Proverb

88. Win with Time Management

Becoming a master time manager is on my list of life goals. Time management, says success expert Brian Tracy, is life management. I have learnt all I know about time management from Brian Tracy, and I highly recommend his books and videos on the topic. His book, *Eat That Frog*, is an international best seller and is worth reading. My life has improved greatly from following the information he provides. I have taught this skill to others and it works. If you do not learn to manage your time effectively, you will not win at life.

Time management is really all about learning how to prioritize and acting intentionally with focus. It is about creating priorities based on your life goals or daily goals and having the discipline to carry them out. Time management is also about planning your days, months, weeks and years in advance—setting long-term goals—and then acting upon them each day. Time management is improved when we ask:

- What is the most valuable use of my time right now?
- What have I been hired to do?
- What tasks give me the highest reward right now?

Without clear goals and having a design and vision for the outcome, it is impossible to manage your time well. Therefore I implore you to learn this skill to win.

Real Life Application: With a schedule like mine, time management is essential. I practice a modified version of Tracy's ABC method of time management and a modified version of single handling to get through my week. I make a list of all the tasks to be done for the week over the weekend or on Sundays. I then mark my "must dos," which are my "A" list and most important tasks. After this, I list the other tasks in terms of importance using "B" and "C." My B tasks are important but not urgent; my C tasks I can delegate or creatively procrastinate on.

I assign each task a due date, and then daily mark my must do tasks on my list of 5-6 things to do. I make sure my must dos are done each day whatever happens. I don't always start off with the must dos but I make sure they are done. This has greatly improved my efficiency.

Key Proverb: *What may be done at any time will be done at no time.* —Scottish Proverb

89. Automate to Win

This is one key that is essential for productivity and financial freedom. To "automate" means to operate in such a way that your direct input is minimal. Something or someone else is working for you. If we can set up systems to run without our input or with minimum effort from us, it will make our lives easier.

Many companies have automated some of receptionist services with pre-recorded messages and instructions so that when you call, it's a machine that is guiding you. This saves much time and effort. You can automate your bill payments, automate your sales through the Amazon online store, automate your responses to emails etc.

This is a key principle to master if you want to become more effective in the 21st Century and beyond. Therefore, I urge you today to think of more ways and means to increase the use of this key in the different areas of your life.

Real Life Application: The bank's system of automation has really come in handy for me. Each month I use online banking to pay my bills and do my financial transactions without leaving my home. This has saved me time and also money as I don't have to travel or stay in long lines to complete transactions anymore. I have also automated payments for insurance and other recurring monthly expenses.

Key Proverb: *Good management and feed give eggs.* —Silician Proverb

90. Be Money Smart to Win

If there is ever an area in life that people need to learn to be effective, this is sure one! Over and over the studies show that the majority of people are living from pay cheque to pay cheque. Jokes abound about our JOB (Just Over Broke) and the reality is: very often it's not that we don't make money, or have money pass through our fingers… it's just that it keeps passing through. We either don't know how to spend it; we don't have enough passing through and we don't generally understand the principles of money management. The problem is compounded even more in that even if we mentally understand it, very often our behaviour is just the opposite. It is for this reason that financial expert Dave Ramsey says, "Personal finances is 20% head knowledge and 80% behaviour."

Having money, matters! This is one area in which I have not for the most part exercised much wisdom. I have paid a lot of stupid tax (interest through indebtedness, bad habits and poor thinking about money). There were seasons when I made too much money to be broke and at my age I am just beginning to see the light, thanks to a decision to become money smart, and just being sick and tired of struggling or losing in this area.

Now, I cannot use this book to teach you all there is to know about winning with money but a huge part of my change has come through reading Dave Ramsey's books: *Total Money Makeover*, *The Legacy Journey* and *Financial Peace Revisited;* seeking understanding about money from the Bible and reading books like *The Richest Man in Babylon*; listening to teachings on money and changing my habits. It is true as Ramsey says, it takes truck loads of efforts to change and at 36 years of age, I am just beginning my journey to financial freedom following Ramsey's baby steps. In this area, if you are struggling, I will offer seven key suggestions for change as follows:

- Examine your mindset, beliefs and thinking about money.
- Listen to teachings on money and study those who are doing well financially.
- Set some financial goals and become a good earner.
- Begin the habit of saving first before you pay any bill—even if it is 1% of your earnings—and increase it gradually and build an emergency fund.
- Give some of it away every month. (Many financial experts encourage giving away at least 1/10th of your earnings, but if you cannot give this percentage, give what you can and gradually increase it as your financial status becomes better).

- Get out of debt and live on less than you earn.
- Live on a budget, that is, track your money and tell every dollar where to go before it goes each month, instead of wondering where it all went. Assign purpose to every dollar.

Real Life Application: Unlike me, my mother has been a very money-smart woman. She mastered the habit of saving and is known for her stance against debt. She has been a giver and a good earner and always has that emergency fund. I remember when I was publishing my first book; it was my mother who first invested in the venture. She is a generous giver. Despite her humble beginnings, she learnt money management principles early in life, practised them and today she is winning with money.

Key Proverb: *In the house of the wise are stores of choice food and oil, but a foolish man devours all he has.* —Bible Proverb

91. Connect and Care to Win

In September 2016, I attended a seminar on suicide prevention hosted by Choose Life International, in which the following were highlighted:

- Every 40 seconds someone commits suicide.

- Suicide is the second leading cause of death among youths 15-29 years old.
- Every year over 800,000 persons commit suicide.

It was at this seminar that that this key came alive in my heart. In recent times, I have spoken on loneliness and intentional relationship building. 1 out of every 5 persons suffers from loneliness. This is an intense state of distress caused by feelings of isolation and alienation, the causes of which vary. Loneliness can be fatal and is akin to depression. Loneliness can lead to hypertension, stroke, heart attack and a number of other diseases.

We all need social support to thrive. A social support system is a network where you know that you are cared for and have persons available who will be there when you need assistance. When it is absent, it is a recipe for disaster. One of the underlying causes of suicide is a sense of alienation (loneliness): no one understands me; I can't connect with anyone; I don't feel loved; no one cares, and life is too painful. There is no hope.

One of the antidotes for suicide and loneliness is to connect with people intentionally to communicate and show care. It was noted author John Maxwell who said: "People don't care how much you know, until they know how much you care." We must care to connect and, if we are to connect, we must communicate by connecting intentionally to show we care.

Many people are hurting and suffering from abuse or grief. Many feel friendless on a planet where we are wired for relationships. We all need social support to weather life's storms and remain healthy as social beings. Let's make an effort to connect and show care today. It may save a life.

The grieving especially need to connect to someone, and this will help them cope. Two grieving wives in one of my seminars on "The Battle in Loneliness" shared their stories. I was very moved when one of them shared that she had a stroke after her husband died, because she had no one to talk to, no one she felt she could really connect to after the loss. Connect intentionally today with someone and help that person win at life.

Real Life Application: I will never forget during one of my most difficult emotional ordeals when my friends invited me to stay at their home in Portland. They knew that I should not be alone in such a crisis. It was during that visit that I was able to review and reflect, unpack what had happened and make better decisions going forward. I have a group that I call my Inner Circle, and when I am discouraged and in need I know whom to call. This has helped me to live more effectively.

Key Proverb: *Sticks in a bundle are unbreakable.* —African Proverb

92. Delegate and Outsource to Win

This twin key is essential for time management and productivity. According to productivity specialist Michael Hyatt, you should delegate something, if you find someone who can do it 70% as well as you. Many persons struggle with delegation because of perfectionist tendencies, trust issues and concerns about quality; if you expand your services and intend to be very successful, you will need to delegate. You cannot succeed alone. Yes, it will take time to teach before you delegate, but in the end, it will save you time.

Outsourcing is similar. It is directing/sending the task to someone else who is more competent and skilled than you are or simply because you prefer not to be saddled with it. You can outsource sub-tasks to free up time to work on your main task.

For example, Amazon is a great outsourcing platform which sells and distributes my books all over the world. This saves me from the stress of delivery and shipping. Fiver.com is another great outsourcing site where you can find qualified persons to do various tasks at an affordable rate. I use them to outsource much of my book publishing process, and it makes my life quite easier.

When outsourcing and delegating, you must act with clarity. Be very, very clear on what you want and describe this in great detail, so that the person or company can follow your instructions well. Author Timothy Ferris, in his book *The 4-Hour Work Week*, covers this in great detail. Read his book for more information. I have seen firsthand the benefits of this twin key, and therefore I am encouraging you to use it.

Real Life Application: Sandy has become a delegation specialist. The job she has been charged with is a job for three persons, and there are times when there are key departmental objectives that she cannot meet on her own. I have watched Sandy delegate and outsource with maximum effect.

Sandy was recently tasked with the job of admitting over 100 students into a particular programme in a very short space of time. The admission process required interviewing all candidates, and it was a challenge she handled very well. Sandy simply called in qualified persons to do the interviews, which freed her up to work on other essential duties.

Key Proverb: *Many hands make light work.*
—African Proverb

93. Earn to Win

Your income is your greatest wealth building tool; having an income is vital for survival. If you do not earn, you cannot eat or pay your bills. If you are not earning, someone else is earning so you can live. Earning does not necessarily mean having a 9-5 job or waiting on a salary at the end of the month, because even children can earn. It means finding a way to be compensated monetarily for your service. It is monetizing your service.

Money is a mere compensation in paper or coin for a service. Jim Rohn, American business philosopher and my favourite personal development teacher, would say, "profits are better than wages." You can make a profit without waiting to be paid weekly, fortnightly or monthly. Most successful persons have at least three income streams.

Most poor people have only one and yet the rich depend on the purchases of the poor to earn. It's just a matter of thinking differently if we want to win. We have to exercise the key *Think to Win* to come up with ideas to earn more to win. I urge you no matter your age to find ways to *Earn to Win* or earn more to win.

Real Life Application: I had bought into the belief that debt is a good business tool, and thus I had borrowed money to do a business venture. I had promised some of my creditors that within six months they would have been paid. Unfortunately, this was not to be.

The sales from the business were not enough to keep the business afloat and pay my creditors. After watching Dave Ramsey's teachings on getting out of debt, I saw the need to earn more to win. In fact, Ramsey encourages persons to get extra jobs to accelerate their debt reduction. I followed Ramsey's advice and secured two contracts, and this enabled me to settle with most of my creditors in six months. This was better than I had been able to do in more than a year of being indebted! Although the extra job put a strain on me physically, it was worth it.

Key Proverb: *The chicken that digs for food will not sleep hungry.* —African Proverb

94. Focus on Today to Win

If you have ever felt overwhelmed, suffered from anxiety, or are prone to worry, this key will work wonders. This key might seem like it's a contradiction to the key, *Think Long Term to Win*; however, it is not and both are essential. Thinking long term is about planning for things ahead of time and is an essential tool to designing a great life or running a business, an organization and a country. Nevertheless, since tomorrow is not guaranteed and we can only live one day or moment at a time, we have to focus on today to be effective.

Today's tasks are what matters in actual living. It is the days that lead to months and years and eventually a lifetime. I find this key very useful when things become overwhelming or when thinking about the future begins to create anxiety. I tell myself to get back to today. I literally say to myself: *Focus on today and get through day; do what matters right now or just for today*. Immediately, mentally and emotionally, I begin to function better and am less distressed.

Is it any wonder that Jesus said, "Do not be anxious about tomorrow because each day has enough worries of its own?" This is wisdom at its best. Let's live in 24 hour compartments to win. Therefore, I urge you to use this key as needed and *Focus on Today to Win!*

Real Life Application: With my schedule of activities there are times when I feel overwhelmed. I remember when I began working part-time, in addition to writing and speaking on a monthly basis, plus teaching online and volunteering weekly. In fact, just writing it seems like so much work. Anyway, to solve my tendency to feel overwhelmed when I think of all I need to do weekly, I began listing all the tasks for the week and itemizing the daily deadlines. This reduced the anxiety that occurred from focusing on the entire week of activities. I then remind myself to focus on my daily tasks and let tomorrow take care of itself. This kind of focus has greatly reduced my anxieties and thus far, I have been managing my tasks well, fulfilling my responsibilities and meeting my deadlines.

Key Proverb: *A good well-lived today makes every yesterday a dream of a good future, and every morning a vision of hope.* — Near East Proverb

95. Mass Produce to Win

This key falls under our resources section, and hence when I thought of this key, I was thinking from a business perspective. As an independent author/publisher, I find that the more books I produce or order, the less are the production costs. Mass production usually reflects the reality of a product that is in great demand. If you are able to produce a product that is in great demand, that is scalable, you will be able to do well financially.

The more books I produce and actually sell the greater the financial rewards; the more courses I offer and sell the greater the financial rewards and also the greater the impact.

Mass production is a way to serve more people and create greater impact. Therefore, I would encourage you to think about creating or investing in something that can be mass produced to generate more income and increase your impact. This is another means of being more effective especially as we explore resources and investments

Real Life Application: The availability of cell phones and computers as well as a whole host of other products from various businesses demonstrates the benefits of mass production. The cell phone companies are profiting greatly financially. Other businesses that mass produce products that are selling prove the point that mass production is a way to win in business.

Key Proverb: *All birds will flock to a fruitful tree.* —African Proverb

96. Network and Collaborate to Win

It has often been said that your network is your net worth. Success expert Brian Tracy notes that 85% of all jobs are obtained through connections. The more people you know, the greater your chances of success and the greater your influence. If you intend to do well professionally or socially, it is important to collaborate and network with others. Once you want to operate on a large scale, you will need to collaborate more and increase your network, since no one succeeds in this alone. The benefits of networking and collaborating are tremendous.

By networking and collaborating, you can tap into more resources and expertise beyond your own. The acronym T.E.A.M reflects the value of networking and collaborating: Together Everyone Achieves More.

This could be done through schooling, involvement in social clubs and professional associations, social media groups, sports, church, community groups, non-profit organizations and other kinds of association. By serving and volunteering, you increase your network and learn to cooperate with others. Therefore, I encourage you to increase your network and collaborate more to win.

Real Life Application: Each year when my church has its annual community health fair, I see this key at work. Each member of the committee uses a circle of influence to get a service group to share in the day's event. My mom being a nurse gets doctors and other nurses to participate as well as the Lion's Club of which she is a member. I help my mom with writing letters as well as with hospitality. Members of the health fair committee get companies to sponsor refreshment, and the young people assist with registration and hospitality. The health fair benefits over 200 persons annually free of cost to the beneficiaries. Without networking and collaborating this would not be possible.

Key Proverb: *A single stick may smoke but it will not burn.* —African Proverb

97. Part to Win

There is a proverb that says, "bad company corrupts good morals," and another that says, "one bad apple spoils the whole bunch." Both these proverbs reflect the reality that not every relationship or association is beneficial. Sometimes you have to part company with some individuals for your own growth, security and upliftment. I am not promoting transactional relationships but merely recognizing that we have to be wise and know when something or someone is no longer enhancing our development. Some environments are not conducive to your growth or health, and you have to leave. The trick is to know when to do so.

This key requires wisdom and courage to part from things or persons to whom you have been attached for very long periods. It will not be easy, but you have to weigh the long term consequences and establish strong compelling reasons why parting would be better, and if it is worth the pain of giving up that thing or that person.

- Will the environment, persons, job or whatever it is create more harm or good in the end?

- How will the association help you to achieve your life goals or help you to serve others?

- Do you have peace of mind about remaining in the situation?

- Can you do more and be of greater value, influence or service if you leave?

These are just some of the questions you need to ask yourself when faced with the need to use this key. Nevertheless, understand the reality that this is a vital key that will be needed at some point in your life.

Real Life Application: When Darby's dad became ill with cancer, she knew that it was time to utilize this key. Thus, Darby left her job and went overseas to care for her dad. Within months of leaving her dad died. It was not that Darby did not enjoy her job but her dad mattered more. It's a decision Darby has not regretted. Sometimes you have to part to win, even if you don't know how it will all work out.

Key Proverb: *Do not believe you will reach your destination without leaving the shore.*
—Chinese Proverb

98. Prioritize to Win

This key principle of success I learnt by using the Pareto Principle, named after economist Vilfredo Pareto, which specifies an unequal relationship between inputs and outputs. The principle states that: 20% of the invested input is responsible for 80% of the results obtained. This means out of every 10 activities, 2 are responsible for most of the results.

The Pareto Principle can be applied to people and organizations. It's a major productivity key. In order to prioritize, you have to ask yourself:

- What is my most valuable task or interest right now?

- What is it that will give me the best results and help me reach my goal?

- Which relationship is benefiting me the most?

The answers will reveal to you where to place your efforts, time and resources. Prioritizing helps you separate the vital few from the trivial many. We need to know where to put the emphasis daily as we engage in activities.

This is a life management strategy for every area of our lives, so that the things which matter most are not given least attention. Learning to prioritize is a skill and strategy which is vital to help you win. You've got to learn to prioritize to optimize your chances of success.

Real Life Application: While writing this book, this key has been tested time and time again. I remember when I had set a goal of writing at least 4500 words each week, and then at work we were given some departmental deadlines in that period which would not have enabled me to meet my writing target. Since my writing career is not yielding the earnings to cover my monthly expenses, my job takes precedence. Therefore, I put writing on hold for a while in order to meet the demands of my job. At that point, the job demands were my priority.

Key Proverb: *The hyena chasing two ga-zelles at the same time will go to bed hungry.* —African Proverb

99. Think Single Input-Multiple Yields to Win

I must admit that this key came to mind when I wrote my second book, *When Trees Talk*, and reflected on the Carambola or starfruit tree that keeps producing fruit every single day of the year. Once again in this resource section, this key is worthwhile when thinking of income and earnings. This key reminds me of passive income. Author Pat Flynn has an award win-ning podcast, *Smart Passive Income*, which provides the information you need to develop passive income.

Passive income is about earning regularly from an investment with minimal effort after the initial investment. There are many ways to make passive income. For example, when you write a book or produce a product or song and earn royalties (a percentage of the profits over a set period), you have created a revenue stream with minimal effort from yourself in the future.

Fruit trees like the Carambola, once planted and fully developed, can survive for many years and produce fruit season after season. If you want to win—especially financially—you should think in these terms. If you want to leave a leg-acy, think in these terms. If you want to mul-tiply your impact, think in these terms. If you are thinking of sustainability, efficiency, and wealth building, this key is most useful.

Real Life Application: The legendary Bob Marley died in 1981 and yet his legacy of music, his albums and songs continue to yield revenue long after his death. Think about it! Bob is no longer here and yet the yields continue. There are even several spin offs including the Bob Marley Museum which continues to bear financial and cultural fruit based on the work that Marley put in during his short career.

Key Proverb: *Where there are no oxen, the manger is empty, but from the strength of an ox come abundant harvests.* —Bible Proverb

100. Work to Win

Recently in one of my classes, one of my students challenged me by stating strongly, "Miss, if everyone is rich, no one would need to work." I of course disagreed, and this is because we have a wrong view or perception of work.

Work is not just something we do to put food on the table and pay our bills. Work is about offering service, and if everyone were rich, it would only mean that we would all afford the service. Even if everyone were rich, there would still be need for doctors, mechanics, lawyers, entertainers and others offering the necessities of life, because someone has to provide such services.

There are wealthy people who still work, for work enhances our self-esteem and may in fact prolong our lives. It has been noted on average that many retirees die within 3-5 years of not working. We don't have to work for an income; we can work for a purpose or the sheer pleasure of serving and enjoying what we do. Money is just one form of compensation for service (work). I believe work is part of our DNA and is a means of fulfilling a purpose and making life on planet Earth more rewarding. Therefore, I urge you to employ this key throughout your life.

Real Life Application: Victoria was unemployed for quite a while. She decided to volunteer her services at a non-profit organization. The non-profit provided a travel stipend, and during Victoria's time working with them, she became interested in serving overseas in Europe. The organization taught her how to raise funds, and this enabled her to serve in England for one year. It was a very rewarding experience for Victoria. If she had had a philosophy of working only for financial rewards, she would not have been afforded this wonderful experience.

Key Proverb: *Igle jackass guh a poun.* (Translation: Stray jackass is taken to the animal pound.) —Jamaican Proverb

SECTION III: ENCOUNTERING THE KEYS

Di house whe shelta yu when a rain, look fi it when sun hot. (Translation: When you become successful, look for those who helped you during the hard times.)

—Jamaican Proverb

KEY TESTIMONIALS

The following testimonials are from participants in my workshops, courses, life coaching and extra mile initiatives which are based on the keys to win at life.

Setting Smart Goals Workshop

I always wanted to own a car, and when Ms. Taylor presented her testimony at my school, it motivated me to accomplish my goal. I wanted to be in a position to see what achieving an important goal felt like. After the presentation, I went home for a few days, thought about what she had shared regarding her goal of publishing her book and how she did it. Shortly after this, there was an offer that I could not refuse and, with the help of my mother, I was able to achieve the goal of owning my first car. Therefore, I want to encourage everyone to set smart goals to win at life.

T. Le-Chin-See
2016 Workshop Participant

Design to Win 101: Personal Development and Life Skills Course:

It helped me to improve my lifestyle and character and to save and improve my income.

—W. Dawes

It expanded my mind and introduced me to a new perspective on successful persons.

—R. Kentish

I appreciate that it prepared us for the outer world which is the world of work. —H. Allen

Helped me develop the mental and social ability to go through life. —N. Francis

It has encouraged me to be more vigilant and focussed in attaining goals by acting on them. The course is extremely useful for building proper goals and life-long positive habits.

—H. Spencer

It helped me to rate my progress whether I am improving or failing. —N. Collins

It opened my knowledge on the importance of saving and to always make a budget so that you can spend for solid reasons and also to make long term plans. —R. Robinson

Most of the modules helped me to perform better and remain consistent with tasks given on an everyday basis. —D. Stewart

My understanding of time-management and decision making has greatly increased, along with gaining knowledge which will positively affect my experience in the working world.

—K. Bennett

It caused me to start thinking more logically and push myself to do the necessary and important things. I have a higher self-confidence in terms of believing in myself to make my own decisions. I now have a more disciplined attitude. —R. Anderson

The topic, "Failing Forward," made me stronger, not to let failure bring me down but to learn from it. —K. Campbell

It boosted my confidence overall towards my social life, work and business life. —J. Clarke

Before the course I was not able to deal with failure and rejection properly. However, when the topic was taught I was able to handle failure and rejection in a more successful way.

—R. Burrell

It gave me clarity on how I should go about my life goals and ways to get them. —M. Hay

Life Coaching

I was in need of direction and enquired with a trusted advisor who recommended Cameka "Ruth" Taylor. There were no second thoughts regarding her recommendation especially because Ms. Taylor was a woman of God.

My journey started October 2015 and was an enlightening one. It was not easy to break the habits formed but it is well worth it. I was challenged constantly to read, listen to podcasts, pray, read the Word (Bible), plan, form good habits and use my time wisely and constructively.

I'm so much more conscious of how I use my time and have undoubtedly seen sweeping changes in my life since my time with my life coach / mentor.

"I believe that people make their own luck by great preparation and good strategy." —Jack Canfield

I highly recommend Cameka Taylor as a life coach and supporter\guide to identifying your purpose.

—Danaé Riley, Coachee

Behind TheSmile Live Event— Evening of Inspiration and Personal Development

Behind TheSmile was a very powerful, inspiring and intriguing event! I received a wealth of knowledge. I'm still trying to soak it all in! It's so much wisdom!

—Andrew McKenley
Event Participant, Photographer

KEY INITIATIVES

Boost your success and transform your life with our life-winning *Design to Win* workshops, talks and courses!

- *Do you have stressful and difficult situations at home, school, work or in your personal life?*

- *Would you like to learn the keys to successfully handle the challenges of life?*

- *Wouldn't it be great to know your life's purpose and have a strategic plan for your success over the next 5-10 years?*

If you answered "yes" to any of these questions, then our "Design to Win" workshops, course and talks are just what you need. EMI will help you, your organization, church and school to W.I.N., at life, that is, to teach and equip you with proven strategies (keys) to help you to:

1. Weather life's storms
2. Intentionally plan for your success
3. Never give up hope and never give up on life

KEY COURSES

Design to Win

Our *Design to Win* personal growth and life skills course will help you to:

- Clarify your purpose in life
- Create a strategic 5-10 year plan for your success
- Develop the success habits and life skills to win at life.

Design to Win 101

This course is named after one of our 100 keys to win at life. It is based on the concept that we have to be intentional if we are going to achieve our goals. We need to strategize to maximize our chances of success. Design to Win 101 is the generic seven (7) module personal development and life skills course to teach you key life skills and strategies to win at life. This generic course has also been modified into three versions to fit particular target groups.

Course Participants
   The generic course can be done by individuals of all ages. Thus far, the majority of the participants have been late teens and young adults (Millennials).

Three Course Versions

The three versions are as follows:

Design to Win INTL: This version is offered to Post Millennials (35 and over) to maximize their potential and actualize their goals despite the odds. This programme will place emphasis on late bloomers and late achievers to show the participants it's not too late to achieve their goals and dreams.

Design to Win FIT: The FIT programme is a training programme for future innovators/-instructors of the programme. It involves a practicum component to pass on the content of the course to at least one person over five weeks.

Design to Win SGS: This is geared towards spiritual growth seekers who would like to progress in their Christian life and personal life. It is a discipleship course offered to churches and Christian individuals. The course places emphasis on spiritual growth and success models from the Bible as well as influential Christians throughout the ages.

Timelines and Format

Each course is offered over 10-15 sessions, for a period of 4-10 weeks face to face, online or blended. The course timeline is based on the needs of the clients or participants individually or as a group. This can be once per week for two hours, twice per week or over weekends for one month. The course has to be offered for a minimum of one month to facilitate our 21-day success habits challenge, which is a core part of the programme.

Course Benefits

The course gives you the clarity, confidence and courage to win at life. Since life does not get better by chance but by design, we will encourage you to D.E.S.I.G.N to W.I.N., as follows:

- **Discover** your purpose and **decide** your next steps in life.
- **Empower** and **Equip** yourself with key life skills and proven strategies, sometimes not taught at home or school, which are vital to survive in the real world.
- **Study** yourself to increase **Self-Awareness** and **Self-Worth**, thereby increasing your sense of confidence.
- **Invest** in others to make a difference in the world locally and globally.
- **Get** it right (earlier or later) to avoid the pitfalls and regrets of others and thereby accelerate your progress personally, spiritually, academically and professionally.
- **Navigate** the course of your life better with the knowledge, resources and insights provided.
- **Weather** life's storms.
- **Intentionally** plan for your success.
- **Never** give up hope and never give up on life.

Course Outline

The course is divided into seven modules as follows:

Module 1: The Design to Win Pillars

>This module introduces you to the five pillars upon which the Design to Win curriculum is built so that you can better understand the course trajectory. In this module we also cover the story behind the course and the objectives of the course and the expectations of those who participate in the course. The pillars are as follows:

>- Life as a Journey
>- Our D.A.I.R. to Win Recipe
>- Strategic Thinking and Planning
>- A Life Design Template
>- Keys to Win at Life [proven problem-solving and success strategies]

Module 2: Life Analysis: My Story and My Identity

>In this module you will reflect, review and evaluate the story of your life, your identity and your brand. We will cover the significant past, present and future aspects of your life. We will help you to become more self-aware and begin to visualize the future possibilities.

Module 3: My Life Design: Decide and Design

>This is the heart of the course and where the actual *Design to Win* plan is

created. This covers your purpose and mission statements, your strategic life plan for the next 5-10 years and an immediate plan for the next 12 months.

Module 4: Life-Winning Attitudes and Actions

In this module you will learn the attitudes, actions and habits of highly successful people which you are encouraged to adopt to help you win at life.

Module 5: Life-Winning Skills

In this module you will learn key time management and productivity principles as well crisis management and keys to becoming money smart in your personal finances.

Module 6: Life-Winning Investments: Investment in Self and Others

In this module you will learn about self-care, total wellness, and personal growth so that you can create the impact and income you truly desire.

Module 7: Life-Winning Resources: Key Resources

In this module you will be equipped with resources to further fuel your success long after the course is finished. These include key podcasts, books, audio, success experts, social media groups and opportunities for financial aid.

Course Cost: Contact EMI for more information. We have special rates for groups and workable payment plans.

Contact Information: This course as well as the key events are offered through Extra MILE Innovators (EMI), which is a personal development and life skills training company owned and operated by C. Ruth Taylor. Extra MILE Innovators equip people to win at life by creating innovative tools, initiatives, programmes and strategies to help you overcome adversity and achieve your life goals.

Contact us for more information.
Email: administrator@extramileja.com | extramileinnovators@gmail.com
Telephone: (1876) 782-9896
Website: www.extramileja.com.

KEY EVENTS & TRAINING

Workshops and Talks

Our keys to win at life will boost your success personally, professionally, academically, financially and spiritually. Once you get a copy of our flagship book, **KEYS TO WIN AT LIFE: 100 Proven Ways to Handle Life's Challenges,** you can contact us for a talk, presentation or workshop on any three (3) or more of the keys such as:

- *Win with the Power of Design*
- *Win with Success Habits*
- *Be Money Smart to Win*
- *Set Smart Goals to Win*
- *Fail Forward to Win*
- *Win with Time Management*

Clients and Participants
   Although we primarily focus on Teens and Millennials, we network with educational institutions, non-profit organizations and community groups to equip people of all ages to win at life.

Life Skills Coaching: This is offered to individuals or small groups to help them discover their purpose and learn the keys to overcome their adversities and achieve their life goals.

Behind TheSmile: This is our flagship personal development and inspirational live event targeting primarily professionals and young adults. It is a forum where successful persons, groups or organizations share their stories, mixed with a blend of a talent showcase, a Keys to Success workshop and tips to help people get their smile back. The event also showcases causes to be supported.

TheSmile is a symbol of triumph, hope, transformation and success and these characteristics represent our mission for the event. Eventually we will be having a webseries in the future to share more stories and change lives.

Contact Information
Email: administrator@extramileja.com
Tele: (1876) 782-9896
Website: www.extramileja.com.

KEY RESOURCES

This section is a compilation of the key resources mentioned throughout the book. Along with the Holy Bible, I encourage you to read or listen to the resources listed below. The resources are organized using the ingredients in our D.A.I.R to Win recipe. They include video presentations, useful podcasts as well as written books and audio books to help you win at life.

DECISION AND DESIGN

Brown, Les. It's Not Over Until You Win. Web. https://www.youtube.com/watch?v=KlUM-rzwmbyo. 2013.

_____. It's Possible. Web. https://www.-youtube.com/watch?v=gXuSMjrx_e8 . 2014

Covey, Stephen R. *The 7 Habits of Highly Effective People*. Rosetta Books, 2013.

Johnson, Inky. *Inky: An Amazing Story of Faith and Perseverance*. Publications. 2011

Maxwell, John. *Developing the Leaders Around You*. Thomas Nelson, 2005

ATTITUDES AND ACTIONS

Bolt, Usain. *The Fastest Man Alive*. Web. https://www.youtube.com/watch?v=E2z_lH3c-s7c. 2015

Canfield Jack and Mark Victor Hanson. T*he Aladdin Factor*. Berkely Books, 1995.

Canfield, Jack and Mark Victor Hanson et.al. *Chicken Soup for the Soul Series*. Web. http://www.chickensoup.com/books

Clarke, David. *Six Steps to Emotional Freedom*. (Renamed: *I'm Not Okay and Neither are You*). Barbour, 2007.

Duhigg, Charles. *The Power of Habits*. Random House, 2014

Hyatt, Michael. *This is your Life Podcast*. Web. https://michaelhyatt.com/thisisyourlife

Jeffers, Susan. *Feel the Fear but Do it Anyway*. Ballentine Book. 2006

Maxwell, John. *Failing Forward*. Thomas Nelson, 2007.

_____. *Talent is Never Enough*. Thomas Nelson, 2007.

_____. *There's No Such Thing as Business Ethics*. Center Street, 2003.

_____. *The Winning Attitude*. Thomas Nelson, 1992.

Ramsey, Dave. *The Total Money Makeover*. Thomas Nelson, 2009.

Schwartz, David. *The Magic of Thinking Big*. Fireside. 1987.

Thomas, Donovan and Faith Thomas. *Geared to Live: 12 Keys to Happiness.* Choose Life International, 2014.

Tracy, Brian. *The Miracle of Self-Discipline*. Nightingale Conant, 2010.

IDENTITY AND INVESTMENTS

Anderson, Neil. T. *Victory Over the Darkness*. Bethany House, 2000.

Ashanta, Didan. *Jamaican Green Smoothies*. Earthstrong Publishing, 2014.

Dunbar, Carla. *Changed: The Journey*. Pelican Publishers, 2014.

Gladwell, Malcolm. *Outliers*. Back Bay, 2011.

Myer, Joyce. *Battlefield of the Mind*. Warner Faith, 2002.

Taylor, Cameka I. *Heartache Queen Un-shackled*. Pelican Publishers, 2015.

RELATIONSHIPS AND RESOURCES

Cruze, Rachel and Dave Ramsey. *Smart Money Kids*. Ramsey Press, 2014.

Flynn, Pat. *Smart Passive Income Podcast*. Web. https://www.smartpassiveincome.com/

Ramsey, Dave. *The Legacy Journey*. Ramsey Press, 2014

_____. *Financial Peace Revisited*. Viking, 2003

Taylor, Cameka I. *When Trees Talk*. Extra MILE Innovators, 2016.

Tracy, Brian. *Eat That Frog*. Berrett-Koehler Publishers, 2007.

GRATEFUL ACKNOWLEDGEMENTS

I am grateful to God, my Life Designer, for His working in and through my trials to teach me the keys to win at life and to be a helper to many. This book owes a debt of gratitude to the following:

To my dearest friends Shauna-Gay Gregory Edwards and Tedecia Powell-Coley who helped me to refine key aspects of this book.

To members of my Design to Win Facebook Group who provided the necessary feedback to refine the keys; of whom special mention must be made of Austin Henry, Davia Williams, Didan Ashanta, Jo-Ann Richards, Kenyatta Lewis, Lisa Sheryl Brown, Meleisa Witter, Rohan King, Shawna Green-Goolgar, Sheril Morgan and Susan Muir, who all took the time to provide much needed feedback during the writing process.

To Dr. Donovan Thomas, Dr. Hyacinth Peart, Dr. Jeremy Griffin and Mrs. Joan Pinkney for your wonderful endorsements.

To my publishing team: N.D. Author Services [NDAS]; Lika Kvirikashvili, illustrator; and Dr. Jean B. Lee, co-editor, thanks for transforming mere words into a very desirable package.

NOTES

African Proverbs
African Proverbs and Their Meanings. Web.
    October 3, 2016. http://hubpages.com/liter-
    ature/50-Most-Important-African-Proverbs-
    and-their-Meanings-Words-of-our-Elders
Afritorial. *The Best: 72+ African Wise Pro-
    verbs and Inspiring.* Web. October 3, 2016.
    http://afritorial.com/the-best-72-african-
    wise-proverbs/
Education World. *African Proverbs and Their
    Meanings.* Web. October 3, 2016.
    http://www.educationworld.com/a_tsl/TM/W
    S_african_proverbs.shtml
Rodney Ohebsion. *African Proverbs.* Web. Oc-
    tober 7, 2016. http://www.rodneyohebsion.-
    com/african-proverbs.htm

Bible Proverbs
Taken from the book of Proverbs and Ecclesi-
astes

Jamaican Proverbs
Jamaican Proverbs. Web. October 3, 2016.
    http://jamaicans.com/jamaican-proverbs-on-
    warnings/#ixzz4M3iprSMU

Other Proverbs
Special Dictionary. Famous Proverbs. Web.
    October 7, 2016. http://www.special-dic-
    tionary.com/proverbs/keywords/reasons/

SECTION II

Decision and Design
1. Rohn, Jim. Web. November 25, 2016.
   http://www.azquotes.com/quote/827007
2. _____. Success Magazine.Web. November 25, 2016.
3. McCormack, Mark. What They Don't Teach You in the Harvard Business School, http://www.amazon.com/exec/-obidos/ASIN/0553345834/purchase-items-20, Bantam. 1986.

Attitudes and Actions
4. Morin, Amy. *Scientifically Proven Benefits of Gratitude.* Forbes Magazine. Web. November 3, 2016. http://www.forbes.-com/sites/amymorin/2014/11/23/7-scientifically-proven-benefits-of-gratitude-that-will-motivate-you-to-give-thanks-year-round/#41761bd46800
5. Maxwell, John. Web. October 8, 2016. http://www.johnmaxwell.com/blog/the-rule-of-5-for-the-john-maxwell-company

Identity and Investments
6. Dillon, Andrew. *Reading from paper Versus Screens: A Critical Review of Empirical Literature.* Web. May 2007. http://www.-tandfonline.com/doi/abs/10.1080/-00140139208967394

OTHER PUBLICATIONS

GET READY FOR TRANSFORMATION

Can your heartaches be healed and transformed into something beautiful? In her mentoring and teaching auto-biography, *Heartache Queen Unshackled,* Cameka "Ruth" Taylor answers with a resounding YES!

This book captures the story of how her experiences of years of heartache were transformed into something beautiful. It shows her pathway to liberation, healing and transformation from many years of struggle with the pain of rejection, poor self-worth and fear. Her heartaches include separation from her parents, two lung collapses, two broken engagements and many more experiences. The book makes recommendations to guide the reader to experience his/her own healing and transformation.

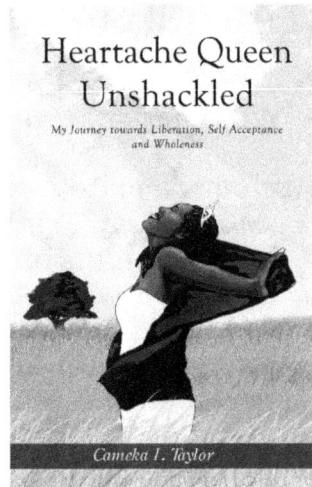

YOU CAN BE AMAZINGLY SUCCESSFUL

When Trees Talk is a compelling and engaging 31 day success journey, where you will learn 100 fascinating life lessons and principles from popular trees. These lessons span generations and seasons of life. This book reminds us that there is no such thing as an overnight success, just as strong trees don't grow overnight. This is a must-read, one of a kind book for your personal development and success.

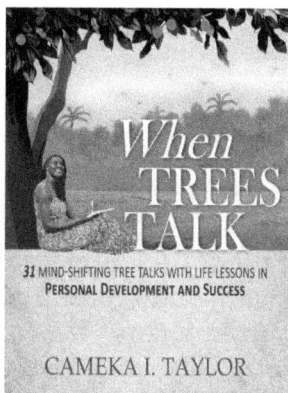

ABOUT THE AUTHOR

C. Ruth Taylor is an educator, speaker and personal development and life skills coach. She is a Disciple of Christ who is passionate about people maximizing their potential and living the meaningful, productive and successful life they were designed to live. Arising from her experiences of overcoming years of heartache and pain, Ruth founded Extra MILE Innovators, a personal development and life skills training company, dedicated to equipping people to win at life.

Ruth has worked as a Career Development Officer, Adjunct Lecturer at the Jamaica Theological Seminary, former Registrar at the Jamaica Theological Seminary, and former missionary with Operation Mobilization. She has been ministering and speaking for the last sixteen (16) years in countries in the Caribbean, Latin America, Africa and Europe. Ruth has also mentored girls from inner city communities and speaks regularly in churches and schools across Jamaica. With the creation of her *Design to Win* and *Behind TheSmile* initiatives, and her books *Keys to Win at Life*, *Heartache Queen Unshackled* and *When Trees Talk*, Ruth's mission to empower people has been further strengthened.

Ruth holds an M.A. in Theology from the Caribbean Graduate School of Theology; a B.A in General Studies from the Jamaica Theological Seminary and a Diploma in Teaching from Mico Teachers' College. She resides in Kingston, Jamaica.